THE LAST THREE YEARS
ITA WEGMAN IN ASCONA, 1940–1943

The Last Three Years

Ita Wegman in Ascona, 1940–1943

Peter Selg

STEINERBOOKS
AN IMPRINT OF ANTHROPOSOPHIC PRESS, INC.
610 Main St., Great Barrington, MA 01230
www.steinerbooks.org

Copyright © 2014 by Peter Selg. All rights reserved. No part of this publication may be reproduced, stored in a retrieval system, or transmitted, in any form or by any means, electronic, mechanical, photocopying, recording, or otherwise, without the prior written permission of the publisher. This book was originally published in German as *Die letzten drei Jahre. Ita Wegman in Ascona 1940–1943* (Verlag am Goetheanum, Dornach, Switzerland, 2004).

Translated by Rory Bradley
Revised by Peter Selg and Thomas O'Keefe
Book design by William Jens Jensen

LIBRARY OF CONGRESS CONTROL NUMBER: 2013952710
ISBN: 978-1-62148-051-8 (paperback)
ISBN: 978-1-62148-052-5 (ebook)

Contents

	Introduction	ix
1.	The Long and Difficult Departure: Ita Wegman's Taking Leave of Arlesheim	1
2.	"I have my hands full with work": The Development of Casa Andrea Cristoforo	39
3.	"Experiencing Christ through Community": Ita Wegman's Spiritual Work in Ascona	61
4.	"Why do all of you distance yourselves so from Rudolf Steiner?": Culmination, Return, and Death	81
	Notes	107

Dedicated to
Dr. Anton Gerretsen

If the balance between the opposing sides is to continue, then there can be no increase in the number of fighters. Remain as neutral as possible—not because it is convenient, but from a love for humanity. Through this action, something will arise in opposition to the war that weakens it and offers something empowering to those who find the war to be senseless. Those who are neutral in this most genuine way will comprise the third army, which has the spirit as its weapon and unites with the dead whose souls have been awakened and whom Michael is leading in the suprasensory worlds. The epochs of wars are over—should be over. Modern wars are simply campaigns of murder. Battles of the spirit are the only ones that should be fought—spirit against not-spirit—so that the living Christ might once again enter the world, not only as part of the human heart, but also as lord of the Earth and ruler of the cosmos. Michael's army and leadership must become a reality!

—Ita Wegman, Notebook, April 14, 1940[1]

My feelings are, of course, that in our time there should not be war, but that the true weapon of victory is higher morality. The greater morality should overcome the lower while establishing right conditions.

—Ita Wegman to Sheila Hirst, February 22, 1941[2]

Introduction

"When Frau Dr. Wegman was there, the future was open."
—Liane Collot d'Herbois[3]

Ita Wegman did not spend the last three years of her life in Arlesheim and Dornach, the cities where she had worked for many years, but rather in Tessin, in the Casa Andrea Cristoforo, which she had acquired back in 1936 for conducting therapeutic work. In this secluded province, which was largely protected from the destructive events of those years and also imbued with a special weave of forces, Wegman developed a great work for the future, gathering, leading, and nurturing people both therapeutically and spiritually, readying for a time when the war would be over—a time that she lived for with the full intensity of her being.

Ita Wegman's departure from Arlesheim, which she undertook in May, 1940, accompanied by colleagues, patients, and children, was ostensibly a response to current events and the conditions they created; nine months after the beginning of World War II, military activity had reached the Swiss border, and the evacuation of the patients, which had been officially mandated by then, was urgent. At the same time, the departure from Arlesheim correlated with a set of inner needs related to Wegman's life story, which is why she also showed no desire to return to her clinic when the conditions at the Swiss border relaxed considerably a short time later. Unable or unwilling to offer a sufficient explanation for this to her long-time colleagues in Arlesheim, who continued to hope until her death in 1943 that she would "come home," Ita Wegman simply decided to begin anew. She occasionally spoke of "many impulses to make a clear break with the old"[4] in her conversations and also in the course of her extensive letter correspondences, but only ever hinted at what she meant. As in all the years prior to these, Ita Wegman kept this question to herself. Of course, she was part of a large and widespread human community that centered on her, but in her inmost intentions, decisions, and choices, she was fully autonomous and alone.

Ita Wegman continued to live for the future, unconditionally and with little regard for social conventions during those difficult years of World War II that destroyed Europe; within the movement, she lived for the prospect of something that was to come: "I feel that something is to come that is actually...not yet here."[5] Ita Wegman wanted to prepare the way for it, but to do this spiritual and social preparatory work she needed distance from the atmosphere around Dornach and Arlesheim and especially from the fatal events within the General Anthroposophical Society following Steiner's death. She needed distance from the people, events, forces, and powers that in the spring of 1935 had taken the leadership in the medical division and the joint leadership of the executive council away from her and irrevocably banned her from her positions at the Goetheanum. Years of unspeakable suffering and even worse injuries were behind her by the time World War II began, injuries that she had long since ceased to speak about, injuries she had completely internalized, but which still drained her. Nora von Baditz wrote of Wegman's arrival at Casa Andrea Cristoforo in May 1940: "When Frau Dr. Ita Wegman moved to Ascona from Arlesheim in 1940, one could see pain and the evidence of difficult trials and great injustice etched onto her sorrowful expression. I saw a great black form in her."[6] Through inner trials and an acceptance of the shape external destiny had taken, Ita Wegman became increasingly aware that she could no longer live or carry out the next major steps of her work in the vicinity of Dornach, and she tried to adjust to this reality.

In May of 1940, but also during the whole period until her death on March 4, 1943, the sixty-four-year-old Ita Wegman was prepared to raise fundamental questions about everything that had been established for the work of Anthroposophy in Arlesheim, Dornach, and other places; these were not questions that came out of critical self-doubt, but rather out of a spiritual openness to the demands of the present and the future, the forms and requirements of new and incoming things. Her last three years were a period of increasing and culminating devotion to Rudolf Steiner and his work, as well as to esoteric Christianity—to the forces of Michael and Christ in the present and future. Hilma Walter, who lived and worked very closely with her in Ascona, described how Ita Wegman, at the end of her life, underwent a clear "intensification of the inner life," and profound "inner transformations of the soul," that, although they occurred in hidden places, also became apparent to those around her: "The power and blessing that emanated from this devoted individual grew ever greater" (Walter).[7] Although she continued to take a great interest in the difficulties of her times and never ceased to participate actively in events— taking in refugee children and the homeless, keeping up extensive correspondences with others, struggling with aid organizations and various agencies, caring daily for the afflicted and for patients and colleagues—Wegman's last three years had a "particular splendor" about them (van Deventer).[8] They stood under the sign of pure spiritual work, of esoteric discipleship, indeed of the path of Christian initiation, with all the forces of conquest and forgiveness that are intrinsic to it. On March 4, 1943, Ita Wegman passed over into death—or rather, into the spiritual worlds—well prepared and with all of the spiritual intentions of a Christian initiate.

—

The following study is meant to serve as a small contribution to the documentation of the last and final phase in Ita Wegman's life, focusing specifically on the forces of the future that emerged so potently in her. Centered on a particular theme and time period, it is a supplement to Emanuel Zeylmans' comprehensive biography of Wegman[9] and presents several ideas that were hinted at in Zeylmans' work[10] a little more fully by drawing on Wegman's notebooks from her time in Ascona and her extensive correspondence, as well as memories of her written by people who lived and worked at the Casa Andrea Cristoforo and several other sources. Not least among these is the noteworthy diary of the great curative teacher Werner Pache who was close to Ita Wegman to the very end of her life and experienced many of the events in Ascona and Arlesheim with her.

All of the documents available to us today display the uniquely confident, bold, spiritual, and social style that was particular to Wegman and that she maintained right up to the end of her life in the spring of 1943. It can be seen in many forms and in many of her actions including her existential seeking, her questioning, her struggling, groping, and presaging. It is problematic, in many ways, to want to use Ita Wegman as a key proponent of a set and established attitude toward historical events and people, as well as institutions, many of which are still extant and active. It is also problematic, however, to identify her too quickly with these attitudes or institutions on the basis of individual things that she said or evaluations that she made, many of which were likely based on a particular set of conditions at a given moment. For as clearly as she often spoke about things, Ita Wegman lived as an individual who served the future unconditionally as part of the moving and constantly changing world of Becoming, and her assessments and evaluations of controversial contemporaries and the possibilities for various institutional developments underwent impressive processes of transformation and maturation. She thought and conducted herself in presence of mind in the best sense, which meant that she readily faced a consistently new set of tasks and possibilities to which she simply opened herself. Many of the passages from her notebooks are letters that are cited in the following text, about the clinic in Arlesheim and the Goetheanum in Dornach, as well as about historical events and the people involved. They are, as a result, contradictory on the surface, and are thereby susceptible to arbitrary instrumentalization if they are taken out of context, and if her spiritual intentions or perhaps her entire being, which belonged to the future and was ever in a state of Becoming, are thereby ignored or overshadowed. It is possible to do this, without a doubt, but immediately one begins to lose sight of Wegman, if not of the future itself.

Ita Wegman was and remained upstanding and free, worked out of the positive with an esoteric Christian orientation ("The Christ is the Christ and fills the Being of Earth only with the positive, quarreling with no world power," Steiner[11]). She felt that she was obligated only to her own conscience and to the spiritual world for which Rudolf Steiner stood and which she served in an earthly way as well. Her path and being were given a clear and exemplary orientation by Steiner's statement that "human evolution will not progress if the Mystery forces do not enter into it once more,"[12] as well as by her ongoing esoteric connection to her spiritual teacher. Whether, in the twenty-first century, these Mystery forces are still to be active in the Dornach Goetheanum or in Arlesheim (Steiner's and Wegman's former places of activity), or whether—according to Joseph Beuys' bold statement—they are more likely to be found in the train stations, is a question that Ita Wegman would prudently have left to the future. But it is also one that she, in contradistinction to all of the global establishments and stipulations, would have felt was up to the individual participants to answer, "Anyone who strives is my friend."[13]

In any case, she practiced and taught a direct connection with Rudolf Steiner in a free manner, centered in the "I," until the end of her life with all of the decisive clarity at her disposal. Ita Wegman's destiny took her, at the very end, away from the distant southern reaches of Tessin and back to the small wooden house by the Arlesheim clinic that Rudolf Steiner had built for her in the summer of 1924. There, at the home of her former work, which she had left three years earlier, she died in the morning hours of a bright and radiant spring day, only a few weeks after sending a letter to the curative teacher Werner Pache in which she described the Christmas work on the Apocalypse of St. John that she had done in Ascona:

> For most of the participants, it was still too difficult, but there were also many who followed along well. One always gets something from it, after all.
>
> As a result, I have the feeling of having finished something spiritually here and I feel that I am free now to return to the work in Arlesheim. This is how it seems to me, although one can of course never know what the future holds.[14]

No matter how one approaches the question of *where* Ita Wegman's path ultimately led and how much the signature of where she died points toward a final, backward-looking goodbye or a forward-looking new beginning, the following pages will nevertheless demonstrate, both clearly and in a manner directed toward the future, the spiritual atmosphere in which Ita Wegman worked until 1943 and also the forces that are still connected with her. Many of her words as well as the whole spiritual attitude and efficacy that were expressed in her seem altogether contemporary and point toward a path to Rudolf Steiner and Anthroposophy that is fitting for both our present and future tasks in a world that seems increasingly apocalyptic and more in need of the Christian Mysteries than ever before.

My thanks go first and foremost to *Emanuel Zeylmans van Emmichoven* for his epoch-defining and ongoing work for and on Ita Wegman that provided a model, foundation and footing for all other studies of Wegman. My thanks also go to all of my colleagues at the Ita Wegman Institute and to Anton Gerretsen in particular, for whom Ita Wegman's Casa legacy has been a great and therapeutic life work for decades now. I would also like to thank Michaela Glöckler for the invitation to give a lecture at the annual conference of the Medical Section in September 2003, which I dedicated to Wegman's last three years and was able to work on writing during the Christmas season. I am grateful also to the individuals and foundations that made possible my research activities at the Ita Wegman Institute through financial support, as well as the friends who attend to and promote the establishment and maintenance of the Ita Wegman archive in Arlesheim and Christoph Oling for printing this book. Finally, I would like to thank Sergei O. Prokofieff for his support of my ongoing work on Rudolf Steiner, which is also expressed in this small study of the doctor who was at Steiner's side to his death and whom Steiner, four weeks before he was confined to his sickbed, had called a "dear friend and colleague in the realms of both medical and spiritual-scientific work."[15]

Only a few weeks after March 30, 1925, Ita Wegman wrote in her first essay for the news page of the journal *Das Goetheanum* about Rudolf Steiner's sickness and death: "Let us hope and be strong and try to receive his intentions from the spiritual world."[16] The extent to which Ita Wegman was actually able to take up this resolution can be seen in her life from that point forward, particularly in the signature of her last three years, the end of her life and her death.

Peter Selg
Ita Wegman Institute, Arlesheim
February 2004 / December 2013

I.

The Long and Difficult Departure

Ita Wegman's Taking Leave of Arlesheim

"*It is senseless to continue pouring money in old circumstances. I am different now—one hopes you are, as well. If we do not destroy the old ourselves, then it will happen some other way. We must grow and move into the future.*"

July 24, 1940[17]

"*As for me, I will claim for myself the freedom always to be in the place where I feel I need to be in my inmost feelings.*"

August 26, 1940[18]

—

"*It cannot happen!*"—at the end of August 1939, these words moved Ita Wegman's soul with the greatest intensity and the strongest powers of thought. But it happened all the same. The war broke out on September 2. I seldom saw the Frau Dr. in such a statement of unrest and despair. She could not bear to be in her room in the wooden house, and in the evening she came back to the clinic. As she moved from her consulting room back into the corridor, she slipped and broke her right [left] forearm very near to the elbow. I received a telephone call about it at the Ochsen Hotel, to which I had retreated with several friends out of a similar feeling of unease. The head doctor of the Dornach hospital was also there. Like all of the doctors in the area, he was mobilized for war and could not offer any aid. But he bid me take the Frau Dr. to the hospital in Riehen that was still partially in operation.

The Dr. was in terrible pain. We set the arm as well as we could and bedded her down for the night in an armchair in her consulting office, and the next morning we took her to the Deaconess Hospital in Riehen. The old and experienced head doctor there was too concerned about her overall condition to risk using a narcotic. The extremely painful operation therefore had to be conducted using only local anesthetic. She had to remain in the hospital until the metal wire could be removed. This was another torture, and during it she held my hand tight in hers....

After she was released from the hospital, we tended to the Frau Dr. for many more weeks in our clinic. The recovery was very slow, and she never regained all of her former strength. The movement of her right [left] forearm was always somewhat hindered. The insurance money that she received for it allowed her to get over it, since she desperately needed the money for the renovation of the branch of the clinic in Ascona, where she then went to continue regaining her strength for a few weeks. She had always had the desire to stay there for a longer period of time. But we had held her fast in Arlesheim" (Madeleine van Deventer).[19]

Her own accident during the period when the war was breaking out affected Ita Wegman deeply. Although in acute pain, she continued to fight actively in Arlesheim against the threatening loss of consciousness in a spiritually tense world situation.[20] Nevertheless, connections weighed heavily upon her during the subsequent time in the clinic in Riehen, when she suffered torturous afflictions, was conscious of the ongoing battles, and was at a distance from her work: "By fate, I was suddenly removed from the most intensive activity, and now, in this place, I simply had to let everything wash over me while I was inactive."²¹ Her first letters written from the Riehen hospital were to friends in various lands who were in danger, but also to colleagues from curative institutions in Germany: "During these difficult times, we are all connected to our friends in Germany, and so I hope that solutions will soon be found for these international situations, but also for the individuals who find themselves fated to be in the midst of this tragic confusion."²² But several weeks later, on Michaelmas in 1939, she also wrote the following, looking back on her own situation and physical state immediately after her accident: "I felt that I was one of the first to be hit, like an invalid from the war."²³

Shortly after returning to the Arlesheim clinic, Ita Wegman shared with her colleague Hilma Walter, who had already been working for a short time at the Casa Andrea Cristoforo at Wegman's request and who was recovering from difficult experiences of her own,²⁴ that she now felt a "great longing for southern climes."²⁵ And in another letter she reported to Nora von Baditz, who, together with Ida Behre, had sent her fresh cyclamen from Tessin,²⁶ that she strongly intended to develop the Casa estate,²⁷ which had been obtained in 1936 and expanded through the acquisition of a farm in Brissago ("the Motta")²⁸ into a small international center, particularly in light of the developments in the world political situation.²⁹

Meanwhile, during the time when the war was breaking out, the Clinical-Therapeutic Institute actually needed Ita Wegman more than ever before; she herself knew that continuing the undertakings she had begun in the name of Anthroposophy and of all civilization was essential,³⁰ and by the end of September, she took up the tasks and problems at Arlesheim once again, including the necessity of laying off some personnel at the clinic that seemed to be ever more poorly positioned and increasingly cut off from the warring nations.³¹

The Last Three Years: Ita Wegman in Ascona, 1940–1943

During the first weeks of November, Ita Wegman was finally able to make the trip to Ascona for a period of eight weeks before returning to Arlesheim in order to do the Christmas work on the Gospel of Mark. This work, which was dedicated to an ever-deepening understanding of the Christ theme, took place every year in the Arlesheim clinic and stretched over the course of the thirteen holy nights. Wegman had inaugurated it during Christmas of 1934–1935 after recovering from an illness that nearly killed her and after taking a trip to Palestine that was filled with deeply spiritual experiences.[32]

Now, in 1939, Wegman, who was still quite weak, had Elisabeth Vreede give the great Christmas lecture on Christmas Eve and limited herself to a short address; but at the end of the year, she spoke extemporaneously about the current situation, the path of inner development, and the activity of the Christ in the etheric body,[33] followed by further lectures that stretched into Epiphany, beginning the new year and addressing the spiritual secrets of the creation story, the activities of the opposition forces and the Christ. Werner Pache, who was working as the lead curative teacher at the Sonnenhof in Arlesheim and who was also present for the Christmas work that year, noted the following in his diary:

> The absolute devotion (absolute and exclusive) to the study of the Christ being seems to be her single-minded, holy resolve. 1934 from Easter to Michaelmas was the period of sickness that made this devotional turn possible; 1939/40 was the accident that apparently made her body more permeable and porous. She is breaking through now.[34]

Possibly from the final days of 1939, there is a notebook entry from Ita Wegman that reads as follows:

The Long and Difficult Departure

Look back fragmentation laceration chaotic circumstances.
Dr. Steiner often spoke of it, was not believed.
Now we are experiencing it.
He appealed to the wakefulness of the soul, to the forces of the "I."
John the Baptist: changes the sense.
Open up to the New that seeks to enter.
John the Evangelist: changes the sense. Something great has come that is connected, with both what was and what will be. Both what is and what is in the process of becoming must be understood in light of the altered sense; then the power will develop to welcome with *waking* consciousness all that is hidden and that is to be revealed.
The waking consciousness, as opposed to the consciousness that *receives* wisdom while sleeping, is what will matter when it comes to the Apocalypse.
Changing the sense means: *making* the *transition*.
Dr. Steiner cries: stay awake; do not let your consciousness be stolen from you.
Thus he is speaking to those who have already made the transition.[35]

Although Wegman wanted to return to Tessin for a second, longer stay[36] shortly after finishing the Christmas work, she was again detained in Arlesheim throughout January and the first few weeks of February. The back-and-forth regarding the disbursement of insurance money that was owed to her—"Fortunately, I have an accident insurance policy that I got once in Zürich and that I had all but forgotten about, but now it comes into effect"[37]—as well as other financial, organizational, social, and spiritual concerns made it difficult for her to get away from her clinic, as she continued to be at the very center of its framework. Most of

Ita Wegman: Notebook entry

her colleagues at Arlesheim were deeply unsettled by the situation in the world. The Clinical-Therapeutic Institute, which had long been an international place of cooperation and the collective establishment of anthroposophic medicine, now underwent an existential crisis. Many of the people there reflected on their customs, contemplated returning home, asked questions about the proper way and time to go about things and fell into emotional and nationalistic moods that made it difficult for them to work with one another.

Ita Wegman worked hard to maintain connections and see to the unity of the place during this period in which the clinic found itself: "I am trying as much as possible to do the same thing here in Arlesheim that we have always done, [which is namely] to follow the Michaelic impulse and bring people together in a spirit of cooperation. This is a very important thing during this period of time, I think."[38] At the same time, she continued to correspond with numerous people of various nationalities from Scandinavia, England, Holland, and Germany, and observed events from a broad political as well as spiritual horizon. Although she had been formally removed from her position as Medical Section director in 1935, Ita Wegman continued to serve as the center of the international movement for anthroposophic medicine and curative education; shortly before, she had taken trips to the therapeutic centers of many countries, making many contacts and staying well-informed of world historical events, against the background of which she was erecting her own approaches and procedures. After traveling in London, she wrote the following on January 19, 1940, with an eye toward the situation everywhere:

> More than anything else, I am interested currently in the world situation, and in how we must arrange our thinking in order to help this world situation take on a form that it

The Clinical-Therapeutic Institute in Arlesheim

must, in fact, move toward, if the world is not simply to end. The salvation cannot, in my view, come from the West or from the East, but can come only from the Center, even if the situation there is so incredibly confused and opaque. The intent and direction of spiritual development is such that the Central Europeans will develop through spirituality and not concern themselves with conquests.[39]

Only a few days later, she wrote in her next letter to England:

> Whatever comes we must go forward with wisdom and courage to be ready to help build the future so that the brotherhood of man with equality and freedom may be understood and come into being through the teachings of Rudolf Steiner.[40]

The Long and Difficult Departure

The destinies of the patients in Arlesheim also laid claim to Wegman's whole being. Although, since her accident, she could no longer fully take part in the clinical-therapeutic work and was forced to give much over to her colleague Madeleine van Deventer, deeply concerned about the spiritual continuation of anthroposophic medicine in light of both the current conditions and her own limitations,[41] Wegman continued to be fully present during the often-complicated therapy processes. Ita Wegman's absolute resolve to heal others and her fully Christian ethos continued to radiate throughout the clinic, filling it with warmth, light, and strength for the future. Although she was not at full strength herself, Wegman's commitment to the preservation and furtherance of every human life was unabated. In January 1940, when an experienced colleague at the Sonnenhof, the forty-year-old workshop teacher Leopold Sparr, became acutely ill, she did intensive therapeutic work with him and was at his sickbed daily. During this period of time, Ita Wegman said to one of the sick man's young and very distressed colleagues:

> You must always remember that every breath drawn on Earth is significant, and do everything that you possibly can. Destiny can change up to the moment of the very last breath.[42]

When Leopold Sparr died in February, despite all of these efforts, Werner Pache, who was very close to him, noted the following observation of Ita Wegman in his diary:

> During the final days of his life, Frau Dr. Wegman continued to say that he must not die. We have to startle ourselves a bit and consider it possible that in an anthroposophist, the power of resurrection—the Christ power—can be so strong that, despite the fact that the process of dying is already underway, a peaceful and full recovery is still possible. She pointed to the story of Hezekiah, who had announced to

Isaiah that another lifespan had been bestowed upon him. Even if Sparr is to die, it is incredibly important that he has not lost the certainty—undisturbed by any doubt—that he always possessed in the most remarkable way.

This attitude, demonstrated by a doctor, is magnificent. Deeply impressive![43]

In the middle of February, Ita Wegman asked a friend of hers, the young painter Liane Collot d'Herbois who was in London at the time, to come to Tessin as soon as possible to live and do artistic work near the Casa: "You can paint as much as you like and meet other people," she promised, and told her about a small chapel on the Motta estate. According to Wegman, this chapel was to be renovated and artistically formed so that it might be able to serve as a place to keep urns:

> There is a wish I have which concerns a little chapel we have in Brissago. I want to bring it in order, and think you would perhaps paint it. My idea is to put the urns of friends who have died there—I am thinking too of myself.[44]

Shortly after sending this letter, Ita Wegman traveled to Ascona, having tentatively taken care of the most pressing concerns in Arlesheim.

There at the Casa Andrea Cristoforo, she temporarily took over the management of the house and saw to countless jobs of various sorts, including a spiritual-scientific study of Rudolf Steiner's courses on karma, which Wegman went through with the coworkers, patients, and friends of the "Casa." It was also during this time that she wrote the obituary of Eugen Kolisko, whose unexpected death in London she had learned about several months before, at the end of November 1939: "The sudden death of Kolisko affected all of us deeply; he apparently suffered a kind of paralysis of the heart while at a train station."[45]

Once again, Ita Wegman intended to stay longer in the south, far from Dornach. She wanted to take up the fundamental medical work that she had planned with Hilma Walter and to develop the Casa further, and the subsequent return to the clinic five weeks later on the anniversary of Rudolf Steiner's death and the Easter holiday was to be only a brief interruption as far as Wegman was concerned. Yet once again, she was detained in Arlesheim by cases of severe illness as well as other concerns and difficulties. After describing the renewed problems with the insurance, she wrote the following to Hilma Walter on March 27:

> There are still a lot of things here that need to be taken care of, particularly things in the clinic that I have to attend to in detail; the problems with the nurses—namely, that they seem unable, in one way or another, to pull through—are extremely difficult.... And the problems related to the medical work itself are bad again, while meanwhile the hope had been that medical work would be able to progress through our efforts; it is easy to feel despair at the prospects of this when one has continually to experience these hindrances that stand in the way of our work.[46]

Three days later, Ita Wegman spoke in the wooden therapy house on the occasion of the fifteenth anniversary of Rudolf Steiner's death and, according to Werner Pache's journal, indirectly cited during this speech a meditation that Steiner gave to her: "Worlds will collapse if they do not hold firm."[47] Ita Wegman was conscious of how essential the spiritual work connected with her was for the historical progress of events in Arlesheim as well as other places. As always, she worked consistently toward the future, despite all hindrances and trials.

On Easter in Arlesheim, she once more addressed the current world-historical situation, the necessity of spiritual perseverance, and the goal of her own spiritual approach. As was often the case, she prepared her thoughts in writing in a notebook; there one finds the following (among other things):

> If the balance between the opposing sides is to continue, then there can be no increase in the number of fighters. Remain as neutral as possible—not because it is convenient, but out of a love for humanity. Through this action, something will arise in opposition to the war that weakens it and offers something empowering to those who find the war to be senseless. Those who are neutral in this most genuine way will comprise the third army, which has the spirit as its weapon and unites with the dead whose souls have been awakened and who are being led by Michael in the suprasensory worlds. The epochs of wars are over—should be over. Modern wars are simply campaigns of murder. Battles of the spirit are the only ones that should be fought—spirit [*Geist*] against unspirit [*Ungeist*]—so that the living Christ might once again enter the world, not only in human hearts, but as lord of the Earth and ruler of the cosmos. Michael's army and leadership must become a reality![48]

The spiritual Easter work, the needs of the clinic, the ongoing communication with the insurance company, and many other things defined the month of April 1940. At the same time, Wegman took an active role from afar in Arlesheim in the proceedings at the Casa Andrea Cristoforo and corresponded about all of the details of the situation there with Hilma Walter: the room assignments of the patients, the quality and cost of the food, and all other concerns of practical daily life.[49] At the beginning of May 1940, she wrote to Walter in Ascona about her "great longing to come back,"[50] and regarding her unstable, ailing, and sickly female colleague, she stressed again the spiritual importance of

The Long and Difficult Departure

. weil die Balance zwischen den Kämpfenden bestehen bleiben sollte, dann darf kein Zuwachs der Kämpfende entstehen. So viel wie möglich neutral bleiben, aber nicht neutral bleiben aus Opportunität, sondern neutral bleiben aus Menschenliebe. Dem Krieg wird dadurch etwas entgegen gesetzt, was ihn abschwächt und denjenigen, die den Krieg sinlos finden, etwas geben was sie kräftigt. Diese, im wahren Sinne, neutrale bilden das 3te Heer, das den Geist als Waffen hat verbinden sich mit den verstorbenen dessen Seelen erweckt sind und unter Michaels Führung stehen in den übersinlichen Welten. Die Zeit des Krieges sind vorüber sollen vorüber sein moderne Kriege sind Mordkriege

Ita Wegman: Notebook entry, Easter 1940

the study that was to be undertaken at Ascona of the health treatments that were practiced with Rudolf Steiner from 1921 to 1924, records of which she had intended to go through, sort, and rework into monographs years earlier with Walter.[51] Wegman went on to say that it might be helpful for this study if both of them lived outside of the Casa and could work together in peace and quiet.[52] Regarding Arlesheim, Wegman put in the following, brief remark: "It was good that I was here; I was able to do some things and to work intensively with people, and that has lasted now for two to three months."[53]

Wegman also made sure that the texts of Rudolf Steiner's esoteric class lessons in both Arlesheim *and* Ascona were fully accounted for, and she issued several directives about this to Walter: "These things have to be kept in immaculate order, because we simply do not know what the future will bring."[54] It is quite apparent that she wanted to strengthen both places spiritually and lead the people who worked there into the future, though at this particular moment, her heart was really more in Ascona.

When Ita Wegman sent the letter cited above to Hilma Walter at the Casa Andrea Cristoforo on May 4, "shooting could be continually heard and felt in the clinic."[55] The town of Arlesheim stressed that in the event of an obligatory evacuation, they could not guarantee transport for the patients of the clinic and the difficult-to-move handicapped children of the Sonnenhof, and they demanded that Wegman and her colleagues give up their cars or place them at the public's disposal. By Whit Monday, the Swiss military had begun to take up quarters at the Sonnenhof.

Half a year earlier, immediately after the start of the war, Ita Wegman had begun making and carrying out arrangements with Werner Pache to move several of the Sonnenhof children to Tessin or Hondrich: "I have sent the sick children away."[56] Now, in light of the most recent events, she decided to completely close

Ita Wegman, about 1939–40

down the Sonnenhof temporarily and carry out a precautionary evacuation. Werner Pache and Dr. Julia Bort went with numerous children to Schwendi near Grindelwald; Helen Eugster stayed at that once-flourishing Sonnenhof, and she was to carry out the correspondence and receive the visitors. By military decree, the Clinical-Therapeutic Institute also had to be cleared out in just a few hours; on Wednesday, May 15, Ita Wegman left with her colleague Margarethe Bockholt, her administrator Erich Kirchner, several other children, and colleagues from the Sonnenhof and the remaining patients from the clinic on the night train from Basel to Ascona.[57]

—

Although she had only just arrived at the Casa, in a very serious mood after days of restless activity marked by great fatigue, Wegman wrote a forward-looking letter the very next day to Alexander Leroi, who had remained behind at the clinic with Madeleine van Deventer, a letter that says much about her spiritual intentions. In it, among many other things, she wrote the following:

> I hope that through intensive spiritual work and connection with each other, we will indeed have the strength to drive this misfortune from Switzerland and make possible this ideal that I carry within my heart, because the whole world will have great need of a sort of global sanatorium, and we must consider it our task to establish such a place here in Switzerland.[58]

Wegman stressed the perspective expressed here to Leroi—that Switzerland must be *protected* by spiritual work in order to allow it to carry out its global therapeutic-social task—again in other letters written to her Sonnenhof colleagues several days after her arrival in Ascona. Later toward the end of 1942, she indicated that the International Red Cross was the most essential task of the Swiss nation.[59] By that time, Ita Wegman, who had grown up in Indonesia and was of Dutch decent, had lived for thirty-five years in Switzerland, that small, multi-lingual country with a strong tradition of independent humanism, a country that had maintained its political neutrality even during the confusion of the twentieth century. Switzerland had an inviting, international, and open quality and commanded a secure state of prosperity that enabled activity. From 1913 on, Rudolf Steiner and the whole anthroposophic movement had "found its home" there,[60] and Wegman, who began studying in Zürich in 1905, expanded her growing medical initiative into an entirely new art of healing in Steiner's geographical and spiritual proximity.[61] At the outset of this new initiative, around Easter in 1920, she had written to a medical colleague that "the whole thing has to start in Switzerland so that it can then be taken up by the *whole world*."[62] Again in 1940, during the time when the European catastrophe was very evidently approaching, she again expressed this cosmopolitan-therapeutic perspective very clearly, even if her hands were (temporarily) tied "because the whole world will have great need of a sort of global sanatorium, and we must consider it our task to establish such a place here in Switzerland."

During that same May in 1940 that sealed the deal on her "final" departure from Arlesheim, Ita Wegman determined the fate of her clinic in her will,[63] saying that it must continue to have, as its basis, the spiritual orientation offered by her and Rudolf Steiner's work and the ideas and intentions expressed therein:

> It is my will that, if possible, the Clinical-Therapeutic Institute, together with its dependents and the work conducted in it, should continue after the course of my life has

THE LAST THREE YEARS: ITA WEGMAN IN ASCONA, 1940–1943

Beginning of the testimony deposition, May 1940

ended. It should, however, only continue if the ideas of Rudolf Steiner, which were the founding principles of the institution, are truly followed.[64]

Somewhat later, Ita Wegman wrote a letter to her colleague Madeleine van Deventer, who stayed behind in Arlesheim and whom she regarded especially highly, providing some context for this statement:

> How things go from here depends on the basic convictions of our colleagues. I want to explain to you what I mean: Dr. Steiner said to me many times that he often thought about dissolving the Society. When I asked why, because I could not understand it, he answered, "People do not come to Dornach for Anthroposophy—Anthroposophy is just a nice byproduct; they come to meet other people and to have a nice vacation—coming and being here have become ends unto themselves." I thought about that many times and about other things as well! And the analogous question as regards our clinic is as follows: do people want to maintain it as a creation of Dr. Steiner and me into which the continued work of Dr. Steiner and myself can flow, or do people want to maintain

it because it is comfortable and convenient to maintain that which already is, and because of the connections between people that have developed there?

If the former is the case, then nothing can happen to disrupt the clinic, just as nothing would have happened to the Anthroposophical Society if people had loved Anthroposophy more fully.... What is to be will remain, and solutions will be found if Dr. Steiner wants to see the work continue. If I am here and not in Arlesheim, then it is because of an inner necessity that compels me to be here.[65]

For a long time, the future fate of the Arlesheim Clinic had affected Ita Wegman. The healing art practiced there was at a highly and spiritually grounded level; yet for many years the Clinical-Therapeutic Institute had been carrying out a yearly, if not daily, fight for its very existence. The political developments in Germany during the 1930s threatened the clinic vis-à-vis its location, but even more threatening were the proceedings in Dornach—one that Wegman increasingly felt to be a war of extermination waged against her personally—which resulted in withheld support, both financial and moral, and indeed withdrew key powers from it. Many doctors in the anthroposophic-medical movement, particularly in Switzerland, took a passive stance toward this, or at least did not rally in support of the clinic or express the personal support, which Wegman had at least hoped for if not expected for the places where Steiner had developed anthroposophic medicine in a clinical setting, places in which all of these doctors continued to live and from which they continued to profit: "So far, the aid that we have given to others has been, all told, far more than the aid that we have received."[66] At the beginning of January 1939, the Swiss doctor Werner Kaelin, with whom Wegman had worked closely for many years and who had both her and the clinic to thank for much of his advancement, retracted his surety for the clinic, thereby putting Wegman unwillingly in an incredibly difficult position with the Banks. She encapsulated her disconcertment and also her deliberations on the future in a letter to the Basel Doctor Ernst Marti:[67]

> I am incredibly saddened by this, because he [Kaelin] has done something that has never happened in the history of the clinic. Everything that had been before that—including the things that came from the Goetheanum—had been directed at me personally, and all of that was bearable, and I could protect myself from it because the work was allowed to continue. This thing that has just been done was directed against the work itself, which is to say against the impulse of Rudolf Steiner that he had placed in this clinic and of which he had naturally expected that it would be carried forward not only by me, but also by our friends in Switzerland.
>
> It is incredibly difficult to give relationships the proper form in this period of time, and so my thoughts turn now to how this work can be brought to a proper and intelligent end, that I might then plant this spiritual seed elsewhere, insofar as it is given to me to do so; or if this is not possible, that I might then work quietly on my own development....
>
> The continuation [of the Arlesheim Clinic] does not depend on me alone; my colleagues must also resolve on it and take the initiative. If continuing the work is a necessity, then sacrifices can be made; otherwise, it would be better for us to look for ways to liquidate it properly.[68]

According to Madeleine van Deventer's account, in May 1940, after further experiences of a similar sort, Ita Wegman finally reached a point at which she would have welcomed an external reason, which is to say some reason relating to wartime conditions, that would have forced her to surrender the clinic: "In her heart, she would have been happiest if we'd had to liquidate the clinic because of *force majeure*."[69] According to Liane Collot d'Herbois, Wegman had already decided in 1938–39 to emigrate to Canada to start a new clinic with the help of support that had been promised to her. Collot d'Herbois reports that it was only the outbreak of war that disrupted her plans.[70] "And so my thoughts also turned to bringing this work to an end in a proper and prudent manner, that I might then—if the chance is afforded me—carry this spiritual seed somewhere else, or, if this is not possible, then continue to work on my own development."

After Wegman's departure, Madeleine van Deventer and Alexander Leroi, joined by the Swiss doctor Marianne Bischoff, did not yield to the threat of liquidation, despite the spoken or unspoken vote of the clinic's leader; instead, they reestablished, within the next seven days and without the army's approval, a complete floor of the clinic with new patients. In retrospect, Wegman completely accepted this development, which she saw firsthand in the middle of June during a brief visit to the Arlesheim clinic: "When the Frau Dr. visited us, she took the reinvigoration of the clinic to be a decision of fate, and approved of it. The Arlesheim clinic had now weathered the worst and survived" (van Deventer).[71] Her approval of this development was completely in keeping with the wisely prophetic thoughts expressed in a letter to Ernst Marti from January 1939: "The continuation does not depend on me alone; my colleagues must resolve to take it up and take the initiative. If it is necessary for the clinic to continue, then sacrifices can be made." At the same time, Ita Wegman disallowed any confusion about where she intended to focus in the future, namely, on the spiritual and therapeutic-social work that she intended to build up and carry on in Ascona. In response to Werner Pache's astonished questions, she wrote to him several months after her "break" with Arlesheim and a year after the state of the war, laying out a detailed explanation that touches on the fate of anthroposophic "institutions" and also on the coming developments in Central Europe:

> The possibility of truly carrying out one's own inner development is most likely...the thing that can sustain our work and that could be integrated later in the great wave of spirituality that must emanate out from Germany. We must be among those whose task it is to carry this spirituality forward and see that it spreads, and with this in mind I have made every effort to follow the laws of this spirituality. If this can be brought into connection with the continuation of our institutions, then that would be wonderful; if not, then one must have the courage to change in order to find solutions so that the development of spirituality is not over-burdened with the anxious and desperate will to preserve and continue.[72]

Very few of the colleagues who remained behind in Arlesheim, at the Clinical-Therapeutic Institute and at the Sonnenhof understood completely what Wegman was trying to express in such words, assuming they ever caught sight of them. Most of them felt overworked and left behind, if not out-and-out abandoned, when, during a period of time that saw a gradual return to normalcy in the region around the Swiss border, they slowly began to realize, during the months that followed May 1940, that Wegman was not thinking about returning. This meant that a large number of potential patients, connections, and financial support were transferred to the Casa Andrea Cristoforo, which had begun to develop rapidly, while the Arlesheim facility was barely able to subsist financially. Again and again, Wegman found herself subjected to carefully critical, inquiring letters, to which she responded only in the curtest manner, her meaning elusive at best and otherwise completely impenetrable: "There is no negative judgment of Arlesheim, but it must be said that what comes from there—that does not pull me back. There are imponderables that most certainly are connected with what perhaps came about through the Goetheanum."[73] Often, she would simply point to her persistent poor health and indicate the need for personal recovery in peaceful Tessin. At the same time, Wegman continued to affirm and fortify those who had remained behind in their resolutions and intentions for the future. She wrote to Erich Kirchner:

> And for me, in the midst of these changes, I have never once thought that the clinic should not continue. It depends truly on the attitude of my colleagues. However, I will not be the only one who deals the deathblow to this work; I would rather go on working in the way that I feel is spiritually right. Moreover, if this work is not properly spiritual, then it will fail, of that I am sure; but if it is properly spiritual, then it will survive this crisis.[74]

Kirchner, who had served for many years in Wegman's name and under her contract as a caretaker and advisor to the curative educational homes and other institutions associated with Wegman's section, asked whether the various threads of institutional development were to be guided from Arlesheim as a central point in the future, under Ita Wegman's leadership. She responded to him briefly, saying:

> The need for centralization will arise when the situation in the world calls for it. The fact that people do not want to understand this makes the work difficult and causes various debates and discussions. I always know that there are no intentions, and that people always want what is best. But I also find that people should have a little more trust in my initiatives—I am in my sixties and can demand that now. In this

period of life one is always open to spiritual impulses, and I listen very intensely to what approaches me spiritually.[75]

—

Whatever was happening in her inner life during this period of transition from Arlesheim to Ascona was something that Ita Wegman did not share extensively with any of her correspondents or conversation partners. Of the colleagues and coworkers who remained behind in Arlesheim, she was closest with Madeleine van Deventer, and in Ascona it was Hilma Walter. In all the years since December 1925 when van Deventer first came to the clinic, Wegman sent during her absences the most direct, open letters to her, letters that never took on a confessional or conversational tone, but always responded to questions about and descriptions of the situation at Arlesheim. These letters, telegrams, and short postcards nevertheless contained notable spiritual remarks, and Wegman knew that these remarks would allow van Deventer to take her into her large heart—and formidable will—understood and reticent. Spiritually speaking, Madeleine van Deventer was also the one who suffered longest after Wegman's departure from Arlesheim and who felt the burden of the clinic's continuation and development most severely. Madeleine van Deventer never argued with her against this departure, but she did describe in extensive and frequent letters to Ascona the true extent of the concerns and difficulties felt by the war-rattled community of the clinic that Wegman had abandoned, in a financial, medical, social, and spiritual sense. These letters moved Wegman deeply and often allowed her to respond openly. At the beginning of September, 1940, one year after the outbreak of World War II, she wrote to van Deventer in response to a recent report about the crisis in Arlesheim:

Letter from Ita Wegman to Madeleine van Deventer,
September 2, 1940

I think all the time about what is to be done. What should be the focus? When I returned [to Ascona after a visit in Arlesheim] in June, I did not find a good atmosphere. It was as though everything had fallen into chaos, and it had all been so good when I left. Bockholt, in the worst state imaginable—depressed, unsatisfied. My domineering and uncooperative Annie anxious, Walter sick and depressed! It was quite a shock. Kirchner only made Bockholt worse. I found it terrible—the dissatisfaction in Arlesheim, the dissatisfaction in Ascona! Finally now, through intensive spiritual work, by rattling long enough of their souls, I have succeeded in chasing away the demons, but one has to ask for how long! It is the same here as in Arlesheim, and it will most likely always be my work to take up the battle with the demons myself. Dr. Steiner prophesied this to me, and so I do not mean to complain about it, so long as my spiritual work does not come up lame as a result.[76]

When Ita Wegman spontaneously decided, only a few days after her September response to van Deventer, to see if everything was "in order" at the clinic herself and to support her colleague in her current efforts for a week, she entrusted the impressions that she gained in Arlesheim in a letter to Hilma Walter, her first medical colleague with whom she had been very near since 1921 and who had been closely by her side during her clinical work with Rudolf Steiner. Ita Wegman's letters to Walter were always filled with great love and tenderness; Wegman cared for her delicate and vulnerable colleague all her life and had the highest regard for her intimate spirituality. She could entrust both the spirituality of anthroposophic medicine as well as the concrete practices of healing to her in a way that she could to no other person. Walter had a deep understanding of what lived in Wegman's *being*[77] and was also able to understand short, gentle, but no less clear remarks. In a letter from September 15, 1940, Ita Wegman wrote to her the following about the situation at Arlesheim:

> Here, things are bad and cold; you freeze on the outside, but also on the inside, for the clinic is empty and the morale of the people is broken. People have stayed because they could not do anything else, because they had nowhere else to go; the work is not being carried out because of any sort of inner impulse. There is no understanding of my departure, but rather a great animosity toward it, as though people are

The Long and Difficult Departure

Hier ist es schlecht und kalt man friert ausserlich, aber auch innerlich weil die Klinik leer ist und auch die Menschen moralisch einen Knaks bekommen haben. Man ist da geblieben, weil man nicht anders konnte, weil man nirgends anders hingehen konnte; weniger aus innerem Antrieb führt man die Arbeit weiter. Für mein Wegbleiben ist gar kein Verständnis da, im Gegenteil es ist Feindschaft da, alsob man es mir übel nimmt, dass man es jetzt weniger gut hat wie früher. Kirchner hält einen strengen Regime was das Essen betrifft, sodass schon überall Klagen entstehen, auch bei Patienten.
Da die, die hier sind nicht genügend geistig ernährt werden, läuft man zum Goetheanum. Nirgends ist ein Unterscheidungsvermögen zu bemerken. Wie merkwürdig, dass alles so rasch in Verfall geraten ist. Und doch ist es für mich unmöglich hier zu bleiben, ich könnte es nicht aufhalten, es muss seinen Gang gehen; es war doch alles was so glänzend schien nur ein Schein.
Mehre Äusserlich hielt alles zusammen aber der Zusammenhalt war ein lockerer weil die Menschen selber keine innere Entwickelung durchmachten. Als ich nicht mehr da war zerbrach alles zusammen. Nun muss man ruhig abwarten was weiter geschieht. Es ist wichtig, dass wir in Ascona etwas erreichen, sonst wird es traurig werden.

Letter from Ita Wegman to Hilma Walter,
September 15, 1940

angry at me because things are worse here than they once were. Kirchner keeps to a strict regime when it comes to food, to the point that everyone is complaining about it, including the patients.

Since those who are here are not sufficiently nurtured spiritually, people are running away to the Goetheanum. There is no capacity for making distinctions to be found anywhere. How strange, that everything has fallen so far so quickly. Yet it is impossible for me to stay here—I could not bear it; it must follow its own path. Everything that once shone so nicely was, after all, merely an illusion.

My being here held everything together, but it was only a loose cohesion, because the people themselves had not undergone any inner development. Once I was no longer there, everything collapsed. Now we must patiently wait for whatever will happen next. It is important that we achieve something in Ascona; otherwise it will be a sad outcome.[78]

Several weeks later, after Wegman had been back in Ascona for some time, she wrote in another letter about Arlesheim and was much more mild and positive, if not more therapeutic: "It [Arlesheim] has not found its way back to its true being. Everyone there must arrive at more clarity so that they can begin to rebuild."[79]

~

Many people in Arlesheim—colleagues at the clinic and at the Sonnenhof, but also patients and friends—waited anxiously throughout the year 1940 to find out where Wegman would spend Christmastime and where she would carry out the spiritual Christmas work that she had been leading every year, uninterrupted, since 1934/1935. As late as September 1940, she indicated in two letters that sometime during November she intended to go to Arlesheim, where she would stay until the spring, but she added the following equivocating statement: "But my plans can also be upset or interrupted, for I must orient my decisions according to the conditions in the world at large."[80]

But after a brief, three-week stay in Arlesheim at the end of October, which was again filled with a great number of activities and difficulties, she decided in November to stay in Ascona at Christmastime, if she had not already made this decision long before then. She cautiously indicated her tentative plans in letters to friends and colleagues at the start of December; for example, in her letter to van Deventer, she wrote:

> It has not yet been determined where I will be for Christmas, because we still do not know where we want to place the greatest emphasis. Here, for example, there are more people who will be celebrating a proper Christmas for the first time. The natural surroundings are also awaiting a spiritual impulse. On the other hand, Arlesheim feels that it has been truly abandoned. In spite of this, one must do that which feels the most essential. Later, diligent work can be done to help Arlesheim, once the borders are open again. Arlesheim will indeed have its former shine again, though that is naturally quite difficult to bring about now, and people are suffering because of that difficulty. There is not much that can be done there now.[81]

As she confided to van Deventer, Ita Wegman wanted to bring many people to Anthroposophy at Christmas; in addition, she wrote, "the natural surroundings are also awaiting a spiritual impulse." She even asked van Deventer to assist her in this work and to come to Ascona for Christmas, which van Deventer declined in light of the situation in Arlesheim. But Ita Wegman did indeed remain at the Casa Andrea Cristoforo throughout the Holy Nights; shortly before Christmas, she sent a somewhat longer letter to her colleagues in Arlesheim, with which she also included a photograph, noting, "This is intended for the future, actually."[82] She then formulated the following statement for the whole community of the clinic and the Sonnenhof:

> During Christmas, I will be there with all of you, and be assured that I am not distancing myself, but rather expanding and enriching, which is necessary for my essential being and will allow me to offer more to you in the future.[83]

In another Christmas letter to Erich Kirchner, whose birthday was on December 27, one finds these words: "May we succeed in being strong enough spiritually on both sides to serve as protectors, that the spirituality which is being robbed from us might not be allowed to disappear!"[84]

Ita Wegman would also spend the next two Christmas seasons in the Casa, but remained in an ongoing close, spiritual, and human-social connection with her colleagues at Arlesheim, and she was deeply grateful for how they enabled her, even though they were initially resistant, to have free space in Ascona: "I was extremely pleased that the Thirteen Holy Nights of Christmas were so powerfully observed in Arlesheim. Because of that, I had the possibility to work here in a way that I felt was necessary both for this place and for myself. This is so incredibly valuable, and I can attest to all of you and to others that it truly was this way. And so I am very grateful to all of you that you gave me that opportunity."[85] On December 23, 1941, shortly before the beginning of her second Christmas in Ascona, she wrote to Johanna Dost, one of her best nurses at the clinic:

> Your dear words have done me good, and I can also say that you should rest assured that I am deeply connected with all of you. I will celebrate the Christmastime here in that spirit and gather all of you in my thoughts, as we so often gathered together in earlier times.[86]

The Long and Difficult Departure

KUR- UND ERHOLUNGSHEIM
CASA ANDREA CRISTOFORO
DEPENDANCE DES KLINISCH-
TERAPEUTISCHEN INSTITUTS - ARLESHEIM
BANK: SCHWEIZERISCHE BANKGESELLSCHAFT - ASCONA
TELEFON: ASCONA 10.30

ASCONA, den 22. Dezember 1940.

Meine lieben Freunde!

Nun schicke ich, anstatt dass ich selber komme, ein Bild von mir. Ich bitte mir zu verzeihen, dass ich das so tue, aber es ist jetzt nicht anders möglich. Ich hatte immer das Gefühl, dass es notwendig war, hier in den Süden der Schweiz auch das Weihnachten mit den 13 Heiligen Nächten zu bringen, wie wir es immer gefeiert haben. Es ist in der Natur hier so - ich möchte beinahe sagen - heidnisch, dass man das Gefühl hat, dass die Elementargeister das sogar verlangen. Auch die Menschen, die hier mit uns arbeiten, haben es nötig, weil sie noch nie so etwas mitgemacht haben. So war es immer in mir ein Kampf: Darf ich es tun? Darf ich Arlesheim allein lassen und hier etwas Neues bringen? Weil auch die Arbeit in Arlesheim doch unbedingt weitergeführt werden müsste und hier etwas Neues entstehen soll, war die Entscheidung für mich recht schwer. Dann kam aber von aussen eine Entscheidung, die mich doch gezwungen hat, jetzt hier zu bleiben, und so muss ich es ansehen als etwas, was notwendig ist. Eine unserer Patientinnen ist plötzlich so krank geworden, dass es unverantwortlich wäre, wenn ich jetzt weggehen würde, weil dann, wenn etwas passieren sollte, ein fremder Arzt hinzugezogen werden müsste. Und so habe ich mich entschlossen, hierzubleiben.

Möge es Ihnen Allen gut gehen und mögen Sie das Gefühl aufbringen, dass wir doch miteinander verbunden sind trotz der räumlichen Trennung und dass es - wenn wir nur alle versuchen, das innere Licht in uns zu erwecken in dieser Zeit, wo es am besten leuchten kann, auch gleich ist, ob ich hier bin oder in Arlesheim; wir sind dann doch miteinander vereint.

Mit sehr lieben und freundlichen Grüssen
in Treue
Ihre J. Wegman

*Letter from Ita Wegman to the staff of the clinic
and the Sonnenhof, Ascona,
December 22, 1940*

Again, a year later on December 23, 1942, she wrote to Madeleine van Deventer, "I will be with all of you in my thoughts, and I will carry you with me at every event and lecture so that I always have the feeling that we are connected with one another."[87]

―

Even after May 15, 1940, Ita Wegman continued to attend in this way to the spiritual relationship she had with the clinic she had abandoned and with the people who worked there, to whom she wrote hundreds of letters until 1943, words and sentences that supported the individuals and strengthened them in their daily activity: "I hear that you are caring for Mrs. Courtney and that you are getting along well with her. I am pleased to hear it. I have always found that one can get along well with Mrs. Courtney if one can simply stand her. You must not take her often bossy tone too seriously. She will do what you want if you can get across to her what that is."[88] There were parting letters when colleagues such as Johanna Dost or Els Eichler finally decided to leave Arlesheim in order to help ease the suffering in their native lands: "Have a good trip! Send our greetings to all of the friends there, particularly Dr. Suchantke, Dr. Behre and Dr. Schumacher. Also tell them that though I have been in Ascona for some time now and will perhaps be remaining here, I carry the clinic in my heart and offer assistance from here so that everything continues to go well."[89] But there were also letters that gave people the strength to persevere at the clinic, to carry on the work during difficult periods and to endure the social crises of the house.[90]

During the first year of World War II, Wegman was more concerned about the social atmosphere at the clinic than about the occupancy of the house, and she was always ready to offer advice to Madeleine van Deventer on this topic: "I am much more concerned about the fact that the Germans, as they say, form cliques and are happy in their hearts about the results of this, thus bringing about an atmosphere that the others will not easily be able to bear. This must be strongly resisted, and if you have the feeling that somebody has this inclination, then it is better to simply break with them and send any German colleagues who are not able to leave aside their nationality back to Germany."[91] At the same time, Wegman already began to develop an idea in the spring of 1940 for the further development of the Clinical-Therapeutic Institute and recommended to van Deventer, for example, that she work with Marianne Bischoff to open a ward dedicated to midwifery: "This was something that Dr. Steiner had as an ideal—to welcome the children coming into the world properly, which would also be about the bettering of humanity."[92] She continued, "If such new impulses do not become a part of the clinic, then the work will not be able to continue."[93]

On the other hand, Wegman gave van Deventer absolute freedom to conduct business whenever she had not offered any specific counsel, and she entrusted her with complete power over directing the medical work. Wegman also gave Erich Kirchner the primary responsibility for the business side of the Arlesheim establishment and all of the associated institutions and properties, though they would exchange multi-page letters almost daily and also have telephone conversations about the difficult economic situation of the undertaking, about tax questions, and difficult financial matters with the Goetheanum, to which Wegman had been in debt ever since her clinic had broken away. The processes that happened there were making matters difficult, if not altogether unbearable for her: "I am not surprised about what happened, because they [the people of the Goetheanum] would like nothing more than to fall on me like a pack of dogs, if they could."⁹⁴ She also wrote about her frustrations to Madeleine van Deventer:

> I never wanted to make a connection between the clinic and the Goetheanum; it was Rudolf Steiner who wanted that, and it was not my decision to build the wooden house—it was built according to his wishes because he thought it necessary for the work of the clinic—and that is the very thing that I now have to pay them for. There is also some crazy B. [Roman Boos] who is ever and again newly permitted to sound forth from the Goetheanum, with the intention of bringing me to an end. Until others realize this about the Goetheanum, the work in Arlesheim will be difficult for me.⁹⁵

There were issues about bond and bank matters, sensible layoffs,⁹⁶ restructuring, and many other things. Ita Wegman knew about Erich Kirchner's absolute, hard and fast commitment and also his great business and entrepreneurial qualities, as well as his shadow sides, of course,⁹⁷ but never let him doubt for a moment that she herself ultimately bore responsibility for the spiritual directing of the Arlesheim concerns: "the clinic, which is to say—I."⁹⁸ This included financial matters and the final responsibility for dealing with the Swiss government—"otherwise we will really get to the point where you were the lord and master of all things, and we would be allowed to do only what you thought best; no, we are nowhere near that point."⁹⁹ She wrote to him about this in a notable section of a letter from November 3, 1941:

> I always think back to something that Dr. Steiner said—that when it comes to the officials, things should really be left to me, because it is a part of my karma to grapple with everything connected with Switzerland. Dr. Steiner said something particular and notable about this. He said that I bore the aura of Switzerland in me, and that I therefore had the opportunity to work, truly work here....

One should still count on me. I am fully convinced of that. That sounds proud and conceited, but it is not; this is something I am out of the deepest part of myself as I attempt to carry through and not to endanger the work of Rudolf Steiner.[100]

The situation that came about through all of this was not a simple one. Ita Wegman wanted her own liberation from the connection with Arlesheim because of an inner necessity, and she expected her colleagues to take an independent and responsible initiative; at the same time, it was clear to her that what she had founded and established with the support of Rudolf Steiner was to be upheld by an inner spiritual connection to her—Wegman's—*essential being*: "It must remain connected with me—if not outwardly, then nevertheless inwardly—it may not be separated from me, because its success depends upon its maintaining a relationship to me, as the Doctor wanted."[101] This course of action disconcerted many people and contradicted all of the conventional expectations that one might have, following the ideas of established psychology; but a few trusted individuals such as Madeleine van Deventer and also Erich Kirchner, who knew or at least intuited the depths of Ita Wegman's *essential being*, had a true sense of the spiritual uprightness of her position, even if they frequently had to struggle to make themselves carry on and constantly deal with the many practical difficulties of this transition.

In exactly the same way, Ita Wegman continued to participate in leading the general anthroposophic study work that had taken place regularly on Thursday evenings and Sunday morning since the end of 1934 and that, in a certain sense, formed the spiritual center of both the Clinical-Therapeutic Institute *and* the Sonnenhof.[102] At the request of Madeleine van Deventer, to whom Ita Wegman had given over the direction of these events, Wegman frequently recommended topics for the gatherings that accorded with her own study work in Ascona. She also objected vigorously when she heard that there was talk in the Sonnenhof of starting an independent anthroposophic study group, separate from the work of the clinic, because of dissatisfaction with the level of the recent gatherings and a desire to orient more toward the demands of curative education work. On August 19, 1941, she wrote to Werner Pache:

> When you write to say that the colleagues there should do work more often for themselves, I agree completely, but I do not agree that it would be a good idea to start a separate anthroposophic evening in the Sonnenhof, because I have always worked hard to unite everyone in Anthroposophy at the clinic. Moreover, I believe that things must continue to be this way, because as soon as the war is over I intend to bring everything together again. Therefore, in response to your query I would say that I do not like the idea of an extra anthroposophic evening starting at the Sonnenhof. It goes without saying that you might offer a course in curative education or therapeutic eurythmy, but all of the colleagues there—and I do mean all—must come together at least once a week to do an anthroposophic work—anthroposophic work that I will direct. And if you say that the work done in the clinic is not deep enough, then it is possible to have conversations outside of the clinic that do offer such depth; and if the senior members are not receiving what they hope to receive, then they should still be present to help carry the work. If I were to return and offer an evening, you also might not be satisfied with me, but I will tell you now that I would not concern myself with that one bit, and I would ask that all who were unsatisfied cease working with me.[103]

In many other places, Ita Wegman continued to intervene energetically from Ascona on still further occasions, and to the initial astonishment of those concerned; she continued to claim knowledge of the spiritual intentions and initial impulses of anthroposophic medicine and curative education[104] out of a sense of responsibility to Rudolf Steiner, who had given leadership of the Medical Section to her during Christmas 1923/24, intending indeed to lead that Section *through* Ita Wegman, and later lead it himself.[105] Wegman continued to live with this esoteric responsibility after 1935 and attempted to use it as the basis of her actions. Without speaking much about it, she acted according to this sense of responsibility and frequently worded her vetoes of various matters as follows: "so that what Rudolf Steiner brought into the world is not denigrated and that something does not develop that gradually becomes separate from me. It is a fact—Rudolf Steiner spoke about this as well—that certain spiritual forces are working specifically to create this separation." Even when it came to medical lectures, which Alexander Leroi wanted her to start giving at the end of 1942, during the period when she was absent from Arlesheim, she declined, politely but very definitely "because I have the feeling that such things should not be approached at the moment, before I have fully and completely connected with the work in Arlesheim." She went on to say,

> You will perhaps find it strange, but I have to take this point of view, because I want to do nothing more that is not borne entirely by me.... It is nothing personal, dear Dr. Leroi. There are simply certain necessities present connected with me and with the Anthroposophical Society.[106]

2.

"I have my hands full with work"

The Development of the Casa Andrea Cristoforo

> "In Ascona, she wanted once again to establish a center of anthroposophic medicine without the heavy weight of what had developed elsewhere. Intensive work was done with a group of younger patients and colleagues. She liked to talk about it as a 'school for human beings.' At the same time, the external situation was very dire. Many foreigners were unable to pay. She wrote to me often about these and other needs, and she bid me, for example, to start taking steps with the appropriate consulates. Her letters from this time are depressing, often heart breaking. But if you went to Ascona, you did not sense this mood there at all. There was an exhilarating, flourishing spiritual life there."
> —Madeleine van Deventer[107]

The Tessin landscape near the Lago Maggiore, where both the Casa Andrea Cristoforo and the Motta are located, laid close to Ita Wegman's heart for years; after the outbreak of the destructive World War II and after Wegman's injury, but also following the previous divisive events in Dornach and in fascist Germany, she could breathe out there after years of a difficult existential battle with powers and forces whose concrete existence Wegman knew well and experienced intensely. The several-week stay in Tessin at the end of 1939 and the beginning of 1940 had already done Ita Wegman some good; but the time beginning in the middle of May 1940 opened up new possibilities. From the beginning, Ita Wegman had glimpsed a great and encompassing future assignment in that southern region, an assignment that was connected with en-christening the elemental surroundings—"Anthroposophic work is essential for this place, as though the elemental beings here have need of it"[108]—and growing a spiritual human society, in the hopes of establishing certain exemplary therapeutic seeds for the future. In a letter dated May, 1941, one year after her "final" arrival at the Casa, Ita Wegman wrote:

> I am happy that I can experience this inner concentration here, with the sight of the lake and the mountains all around me and the wonderfully beautiful nuances of color seen at sunrise, free from the unrest of all the greater events happening in the world. This is a blessing and grace, but at the same time, it is a duty carried out for the future, of that I am very aware. [109]

In countless other messages from 1940 to 1943, Ita Wegman reported to friends and acquaintances how well and healthy she was feeling since arriving in Ascona. For example, on May 19, 1940, she had already written, "I am completely astonished at how strong I have become here and how little illness I have experienced here. I have never felt so good in my life."[110] She described again and again how completely the forces of the landscape, the atmosphere, and the climate of that special area affected her, writing in August 1942 to Jules Sauerwein in Paris:

> What I like so very much and what makes such a great impression on me is the climate; it is the same climate that I experienced in Greece: the expanse of blue on the horizon, across

"I have my hands full with work"

Casa Andrea Cristofaro

the sky and the mountains, and then the deep blue water with the green islands floating in it, the vegetation, the alternation of warmth and breeze, and the light, the complete changes that it undergoes here. Everything here inspires you to create something, whether artistic or spiritual-scientific.[111]

In other letters, she hints at the fact that the surroundings of the Casa remind her of the mountain landscape of her childhood in Indonesia, and how much good the bright warmth does for her ("For me, since I was once in India [Indonesia], the climate is ideal."[112]), as well as the siliceous rock formations,[113] in contrast to Dornach's chalk formations, particularly in the interplay of Tessin's changing light. In a letter to Helen Eugster from her first Christmas in Ascona, she wrote, "When the sun shines bright and clear, and you can catch the moment when it sets, it calls up a memory that is so similar to the atmosphere in Palestine on the sea of Gethsemane. This is more what the experiences are like that one has here at this time."[114]

In September 1911, Rudolf Steiner had held two special lectures in Tessin; on September 19, 1911, he had spoken in Lugano, "on the peaceful mountains and in sight of the wonderful lake,"[115] about how spiritual changes in the essential processes of nature and their relationship to human beings would happen during the twentieth century. The content of these lectures meant a lot to Ita Wegman and was deeply connected with her inner biography, as well as her therapeutic work during the twentieth century.[116] Now she would be living for a longer period in that area, she looked into its history[117] and studied its deep constitution, immersing herself in this region that she wanted to lead into the future.

―

During the spring of 1940 sixteen patients lived in the Casa Andrea Cristoforo and several nearby residences that Ita Wegman had rented, as well as fifty children in the Motta, half of whom came from the Sonnenhof in Arlesheim. Ita Wegman dedicated herself to them and to other children, youths, and adults who increasingly found their way to her until February 21, 1943, the day of her last departure to Arlesheim: "One does everything that a person can to protect the people who are entrusted to you."[118] War-rattled children with particular paths of incarnation and life, adults experiencing biographical crises, Jewish refugees and homeless people, people who were bodily ill or dying, but also those convalescing or in recovery, all came to her in Tessin, seeking her presence and advice during the years of World War II. "The patients truly need a complete transformation, if they want to be healthy enough to be able to incarnate properly in their next lives," Wegman wrote as early as October 4, 1939, to her colleague Ludwig Engel in London with her eye toward the Casa.[119] Now she emanated her work outward from this special place, drawing on the full power of her therapeutic being and working against all the threats of the times: "You saw Dr. Wegman's great figure everywhere—she would walk in with rapid steps, and with an encouraging smile she would radiate love. She helped to keep all aspects of this bustling life in order" (Nora von Baditz[120]); Wegman herself had stressed, in a letter to Nora von Baditz written in Arlesheim during the preceding year that "there is a spiritual wish for us to pull through."[121]

Ita Wegman was familiar with people and with their destinies, but also with the great dark and evil things that were part of the fates of the twentieth century and the lives of individuals who lived in it. She tried, to an unusually great extent and with a great intensity—but one that never encroached upon the individual's freedom—to lead people on a soul level, supporting and encouraging them on their inner paths.[122] She guided from afar many of her former Arlesheim patients, but also other events and moments in life, such as births and baptisms,[123] illnesses, and deaths[124] with great intensity and loyalty: "All those who are my patients are always alive in my consciousness."[125] Among them were countless colleagues, friends, and acquaintances in need who were unable to travel to her in Tessin but still requested her counsel. Wegman herself had experienced much darkness in the last few years and had come through upright and unbroken, which many people around her sensed or intuited; the emanation of her being and the power of her words had grown even greater, and many of her encouraging letters of advice resonate with the deep tones of someone who has lived through much:

> Do not let yourself be discouraged! It is much more important to be and to stay healthy. We have received so many blows, and we have always recovered. Such a crisis must always be reckoned against the whole course of a life, and it often has a seed of something good hidden within it.[126]

The atmosphere that Ita Wegman spread and protected around herself in Ascona was filled with living, moving, and therapeutic qualities,[127] and it enveloped not only the people, but also the natural world of plants and animals, therapeutic herbs, and even the cats.[128] The healing art practiced by Ita Wegman—in opposition to all of the threats of that epoch, which she faced with courage and resolution[129]—was, at its very core, eminently Christian in its essence, imbued with and substantiated by forces of sacrifice and transformation. In the words of Liane Collot d'Herbois:

> She was aware of and emphasized the fact that the qualities of the human heart and its future development could be hampered in a very short period of time, and with that in mind, she directed her attention toward everything connected with healing and recovery—a sort of healing that radiated warm, caring, supportive forces.... Dr. Wegman's ideal, which Dr.

Ita Wegman with Maria and Monika Muller, summer 1942

Walter shared, was a public clinic (which was unrealizable during that period of time) for all people in which the force of devotion (to which she always spoke of giving her life) was utilized as a force of healing.[130]

―

"Do not be angry with me because I have this practical sense. In the end, whether we are able to carry on is dependent on this same practical sense," Ita Wegman wrote in a letter in late 1940.[131] She took care of everything herself, from the heating of the Casa to the most affordable options for gathering paper and briquettes during times of need. She went to trade markets to inspect different varieties of ovens for the building, saw to an efficient system for handling wash at the Casa, dealt with the necessary repairs to the car and with the acquisition of gasoline credits, not to mention the complicated processes of obtaining legal permits and difficult visas or permissions to stay in the country for her colleagues and patients "because it is a matter of doing these various things in the spiritual present before chaos has time to develop."[132] She also wrote long and detailed letters almost every day, so that through medical documents and records of treatment, many of her curative education patients who came from National Socialist Germany and who might have been endangered if they were to return might be able to stay in Switzerland under her custody. She fought for financing for children and adult patients who had long since been cut off from their relatives and homelands by the war and were living at the expense of the Casa and, for a time, she had absolutely no means of providing for herself. She was "poor as a church mouse," she wrote on January 23, 1943 to Erich Kirchner five weeks before her death.[133] Her financial situation did not prevent her from continuing to do what was right, good, and necessary with all of her energy:

> In spite of that, I am not depressed or without hope, because I know perfectly well that we have to be there, that what we are doing and also everything that is connected with me has to be exactly as I have done it, and that the money really should not play such a large role—although one does need money.
>
> So I am also conscious and of the fact—and do not doubt it for a minute—that when things really go in the way that they are intended to go spiritually, there will not be a shortage of money. I must simply continue to place the spiritual in the foreground and cannot be hampered in my spiritual activity.[134]

Wegman saw to it that war-ravaged children who had found refuge in Switzerland with the assistance of the International Red Cross could come to the Motta and receive excellent care, supervision, and "spiritual guidance,"¹³⁵ and she conducted a very successful donation campaign among anthroposophists, friends of the Arlesheim clinic and former patients. She organized Christmas bazaars and attended to every detail—the pieces of handicraft and the book-presence, the pictures, and marionette plays—but in the midst of the war, she also recommended to an overworked and depressed colleague at the Motta that she take a vacation to the city: "I think it would be good to free her up completely from everything for a week or fourteen days and send her to the city, where she can immerse herself in art and other things."¹³⁶ Wegman herself went on interesting and typical (for her) excursions in Ascona¹³⁷ and disappeared suddenly in spring 1942 for a few days to Zurich,¹³⁸ where she had once studied and worked, visiting the festival there and seeing the "Twilight of the Gods," the "Orestae," the "Storm," and the "Maiden of Orléans": "You experience it with her when Joan of Arc journeys into the spiritual world after dying—you experience what every soul must undergo in the spiritual world after death. Terribly fascinating!"¹³⁹

Together with Hilma Walter—with whom she lived outside of the Casa and who prepared her own medications for the Casa and the Motta—Ita Wegman went through the medical case histories from 1921 to 1924 and reimmersed herself in the practices of anthroposophic medicine originally introduced by Rudolf Steiner. Wegman had a deep concern not only for the external demands of this healing art, but also for its inner substance, which had to be constantly cared for, which is to say, one had to immerse oneself in it and internalize it. In the years following Rudolf Steiner's death, the anthroposophic medicine movement had, without question, grown substantially and become very successful and active therapeutically, but it did not escape Ita Wegman's notice that certain elements of the tradition, a certain pragmatism, and a general flattening of the medical art had begun to establish themselves. For years in her work at Arlesheim, she had looked for ways to avoid this tendency, which she felt inwardly to be a distancing from Steiner and the New Mysteries. In the special surroundings of Tessin, where she enjoyed greater freedom and was working together personally with Hilma Walter ("who still carries everything given by Doctor [Steiner] livingly within her"[140]), beginning in 1940, Wegman could finally take up the work that she had wanted to do for so long[141] and gave herself assignments related to it:

> She sought out a new meaning of healing that brings therapeutic energy to bear against the damages done to the child's nervous system by the horrors and shock of war. She succeeded, with the help of earlier indications given by Rudolf Steiner, in developing such a practice.[142]

With the help of several people, Wegman was simultaneously able to develop the Casa Andrea Cristoforo itself into a place ever more oriented toward the healing arts. In the midst of a world that was destroying itself, Wegman created the seed for a medical-therapeutic, cultural, and humanistic new beginning; she and Nora von Baditz offered eurythmy courses, ordered lyres from Lothar Gärtner in Constance and organized concerts by Edmund Pracht and Walter Rummel, as well as excellent puppet plays by Werner Pache who traveled there specifically to offer them. Together with Liane Collot d'Herbois (whom she had tried for many years to free up so that she could practice painting, even taking her out of a curative education job in England for that reason[143]), Ita Wegman enabled the development of art and painting therapeutic practices within the Casa Andrea Cristoforo, the likes of which had never been known before. Wegman herself regularly held lectures on art history, complete with slides, for the patients and friends of the Casa[144]—evening lectures for which she requested, at the end of

1940, that her projection screen be sent from the wooden house in Arlesheim. Ita Wegman also spent a lot of time with Collot d'Herbois's images, including those still in development and those intended for specific patients or particular rooms. She told her:

> Your paintings must be healing. That is what it means to say that an image means something to a particular individual or an institution. That it reminds people of the spiritual world.[145]

In another memory of her experiences with Ita Wegman in Ascona, Collot d'Herbois wrote:

> Images meant a great deal to her and could move her powerfully. A painting was capable of completely changing a decision she had made in one direction or another. I am thinking for example of an image of John the Baptist—she stood in front of it and said, "I am astounded..." and already, certain decisions she had made were completely changed.
>
> She always judged an image first on its therapeutic qualities. Sometimes she looked for the *"Michaelic light."* She was hardly ever—if ever—satisfied by simply the content of the image. An image was more to her than just an image; she could become inflamed with great enthusiasm about them.
>
> It happened in the last winter before she died. She was weighed down by all of the limitations placed on her work, and she saw the danger that was hanging threateningly over humanity. In her own words, she said that she "felt cut off from the spiritual world." Then a new painting was brought before her, and suddenly she sprang up, full of fire and awareness, and she cried, "The spiritual *is* here! The connection to the spiritual world is reestablished!"[146]

By the time of the first Michaelmas in 1940, Ita Wegman was already very set on having certain paintings by Liane Collot d'Herbois on the walls of the Casa Andrea Cristoforo, and during a brief absence, she sent the following words to Anni Viehoff: "Humanity needs this [exhibition], but we must also offer a means of entry for the spiritual beings to connect with us."[147]

―――

One or two times a week, Ita Wegman rode with the mail car to the Motta, which was attended to from a medical perspective the rest of the time by Margarethe Bockholt. The children and youth who lived there were very close to Ita Wegman. She had known many of them for years, through all of their challenges and their stages of development, indeed in the whole course of their destinies, and she also corresponded regularly from Ascona with their parents, describing courses of development, difficulties, and hopes. In the spring of 1941, Ita Wegman surprisingly shared with the astounded and initially disconcerted Werner Pache—to whom she always animatedly reported about her experiences with the Motta children, both special ones and the everyday[148]—that several of the children who moved from Arlesheim to Brissago would not be returning to the Arlesheim Sonnenhof, even though there was space there and no danger anymore, for, she said, they were "karmically connected" with her.[149]

Wegman's weekly visits to the children at the workshops and grounds of the Motta were a high point of the already very colorful and flourishing life there.[150] However, they also meant a great deal to Ita Wegman and indirectly to the Casa and the people living there:

> Upon returning to the Casa Andrea Cristoforo in Ascona, she [Ita Wegman] was only more exuberant, talking at the table about the children with the deepest heartfelt warmth. No one could remain all that depressed in her presence—her words and images were like beams of sunlight. (Baditz[151])

"I have my hands full with work"

At the same time, Ita Wegman continued to take part in all of the proceedings at the Arlesheim Sonnenhof, calling frequently and exchanging detailed letters several times a week with Werner Pache, letters concerned with the cares and needs of the curative education institute as well as with the very particular development of individual children. On her first birthday in Ascona, on February 22, 1941, when she turned sixty-five, she received a large packet from the Sonnenhof in Arlesheim that had been assembled by all of the children whom Ita Wegman loved and honored, and who had experienced over the years how well she knew and took seriously each and every one of them. In Wegman's thank-you note to Werner Pache, she wrote six days later:

> I was...very happy to see the beautiful drawings by the children—I find all that very moving. The writing samples interested me greatly. I was happy to see that Cora can write so well. The beautiful snowdrop image by Klein-Vreneli and little sister Esther brought me great joy, as did the actual one that was sent to me from the Sonnenhof garden. Lucie has made a lot of progress—you can see that in her picture and in her handwriting. And Suzanne, who wants to go to America, also did beautifully in her writing sample. I was also happy to see Alwin's little picture. Alan's conception of Brissago and Arlesheim was incredibly interesting and amusing to me. But he really has the right sense of it—the mountains with the blue sky and the red that comes up from the bottom; they are probably little boats that he saw on the water. I think that he understood the contrast between Brissago and Arlesheim very well. I find the domestic life in Arlesheim, by contrast, to be absolutely charming. Send my heartfelt greeting to all of the children and tell them that it made me so happy to have them think of me. The fact that poor Elma is still confined to her bed makes me very sad. One hopes that she will start to feel better. Send her my greetings as well.[152]

The Last Three Years: Ita Wegman in Ascona, 1940–1943

A few weeks earlier, Ita Wegman had sent a lengthy letter to the orphaned Bendit Loeb, a blind Jewish boy whose development was very retarded, after she had learned that his grandfather—the only family that the boy had left—who had brought him several years ago to the Sonnenhof and who supported and guided him from a distance,[153] had died unexpectedly. This letter from Ascona reads:

> Ascona, January 27, 1941
>
> My dear Ben!
> I have heard that your dear grandfather suddenly died. I was very sad to hear this, because it is always sad when you can no longer have an experience of someone you love on the Earth. But you know, dear Ben, that the soul of your dear grandfather lives on and has now moved surely in the spheres of Dr. Steiner, because Dr. Steiner gathers everyone who has any connection with us, which your grandfather did because he sent you to us. So let us not be sad about this. Things will be good for him now, and you must do everything you can to make sure that you progress in your own development. Nurse Sidonie and your wonderful teacher Herr Dörfler will see to that. I am always with you in my thoughts and am filled with joy at every step forward that you are able to take.
> I was very happy to receive your letter and the little picture that you made on your birthday.
> Be brave and good! We are all thinking of you with love.
>   Faithfully
>   Your
>   Dr. I. Wegman[154]

On the same day, in a longer letter to Nurse Sidonie, Ben's caretaker at the Sonnenhof, Wegman wrote the following reflective sentences: "It is not beautiful in the world right now; people are agitating against the Jews everywhere now, and no one knows where that will lead."¹⁵⁵

Even in Ascona, Ita Wegman took part with an alert and critical attention in the dramatic political and military developments that were shaking the European continent and many other regions of the world; although she was doing therapeutic work locally, establishing and readying things on a small scale and completely on her own terms, Wegman nevertheless remained in constant connection with these larger transformative world events. She could only discuss these things with a few friends who were spiritually minded like her: "We, in our small circle, try to assess things from our perspective."¹⁵⁶ These were people such as *The Matin* editor Jules Sauerwein, who was an occasional guest in Ascona, to whom she wrote, "It might also be necessary, my dear Herr Sauerwein, for us to have some time alone to speak about the political future, because as students of Rudolf Steiner, something will also be asked of us."¹⁵⁷ She also was able to talk with decidedly few of her anthroposophic doctor colleagues: "I would much like to talk with you [Mr. Kaelin] about the situation in the world, because there are unbelievably great problems there, and as anthroposophists—as students of Dr. Steiner—we must have a proper picture of the world within us."¹⁵⁸ Otherwise, Wegman was largely alone, suffering from the burden of the catastrophic developments that she saw or anticipated, and from her remote isolation in Switzerland as well: "For those of us who are accustomed to feeling at home all over the world, this sort of forced imprisonment in Switzerland is very hard to bear."¹⁵⁹ She felt a "sense of being blown apart and separated" from her international friends who had taken the anthroposophic-therapeutic initiatives to countless other countries: "because I carry relationships to the whole world far too much within myself."¹⁶⁰ At the same time, she wrote to a former patient in Sweden:

The Last Three Years: Ita Wegman in Ascona, 1940–1943

One must wait patiently to see how these matters will be decided and remain distant from any sympathies or antipathies for one group or another, because the world must be cured of all these feelings of hatred that are circulating everywhere; neutrality—true, genuine neutrality toward everything—is the first principle of a proper conception of Christianity. As anthroposophists, we must awaken such healing thoughts and feelings in ourselves, that a start may be made somewhere. So take courage. Sweden and Switzerland may have a great task before them in the future.[161]

Ita Wegman never complained: "What is happening in the world right now is so sad. But it is no great surprise; humanity has done everything that brought it to destruction."[162] Instead, whenever and wherever the conditions of the war and the state of communications would allow for it, she maintained an active international correspondence for years with others in the anthroposophic-medical movement, such as with the curative education institute of the Russian Vala Nikitina Vachadzé-Bérence, which had relocated from Nazi-held Paris and Courcelles to a farm in the southern part of France and received support from Wegman.[163] There were also curative educators in England and Iceland, as well as occasional communications with the Camphill founder Karl König, who had fled to Scotland, where he was temporarily detained. "In any case, it is impossible in these times to write things which lie deep at heart," she wrote in one sentence in English to König, hinting at many things she might have wanted to say.[164] Ita Wegman knew that both she and her anthroposophic activities were thoroughly followed, consciously and alertly, by the German powers: "I, too, as Dr. Ita Wegman, am on the black list; people are informing on me."[165] In Arlesheim, she urgently indicated to Nurse Wilma Kröncke in the fall of 1941 that her entire correspondence with Gnadenwald should be burned as quickly as possible, because the sanatorium[166] there—which was so important to her and had been set up for the therapeutic "path to the East"—had been occupied by the National Socialists, and the colleagues there had been temporarily imprisoned. From that point on, and against this backdrop, Ita Wegman was very reserved in her written correspondence with her many German friends, and whenever possible, she let the returning nurses (like Johanna Dost) convey her greetings by word of mouth. When one of the "last faithful friends" in Arlesheim, Nurse Katja Brühl, obtained a visa for a visit to Germany in August 1941, Wegman promptly sent her a longer letter at the clinic, which read:

> I have intentionally chosen not to write recently so as not to create a difficult situation for anyone, but I long for news and worry for the Archduke Georg Mortiz, for Hauschka, Stavenhagen, Frau Dr. Hartmann, worry for Gnadenwald and the friends who live there. I should know *much* about Dr. Behre, Suchantke, Nurse Johanna, the [curative education] institutes, our friends in Stuttgart, Schumacher. I should know everything concerning Germany—my heart bleeds for that people, whom I love.[167]

Indeed, Ita Wegman was concerned constantly with Germany's path and destiny ("I am connected with my entire soul to the fate of Germany"[168]). As certain, direct, and unerring as Wegman was for many years in her assessment of National Socialism,[169] she hoped just as strongly that the country, with all of its spiritual possibilities, would not collapse completely in all of the catastrophes that it had initiated, but would find a way to undergo "an inner metamorphosis in defense," as she wrote to Werner Pache following the horrifying battle of Stalingrad.[170] As early as the summer of 1941, she had written to Erich Kirchner:

> I think day and night about how one should conduct oneself in relation to all of these things and how best to remain

connected with Germany and fend these things off without falling under the wheels oneself. Germany must get a hold of itself again and end this war, independent of the system that has nothing to do with the German spirit. There are strange connections present that must absolutely be understood if we hope to assess properly the complicated events currently happening in the world.[171]

She consistently and ever more frequently received news in Ascona of fallen friends, former patients, and relatives. There were also occasional indications that the German army might, in fact, press into Italy through Switzerland, which also meant through Tessin, provided that certain political upheavals took place there.

Late in the summer of 1942, Hanna Lissau, Wegman wrote of a Viennese eurythmist and curative teacher of Jewish descent who had begun training at the Sonnenhof in 1932 and who, much to Ita Wegman's confusion,[172] had gone from there to Paris to Vala Nikitina Vachadzé-Bérence in December 1939: "In regard to Fräulein Lissau, I am very sad that she will be leaving the Sonnenhof just before Christmas and heading out into the world during these difficult times."[173] The French police, who were cooperating with the National Socialists, traced Lissau to the small institute in southern France and deported her to a place "whose location no one knows.[174] In early September 1942, Ita Wegman received this news from Werner Pache during a period when she had placed all of her hopes on being able to bring forty children to the Sonnenhof through the Red Cross, an effort that had ultimately failed, owing in no small part to internal difficulties in Arlesheim. Embittered and disappointed by Helen Eugster's and Werner Pache's conduct in this matter,[175] she was then informed on September 7 of Hanna Lissau's deportation. That same day, she wrote a letter to Madeleine van Deventer:

Unfortunately, Pache rejected the—in my opinion, exceptional—recommendation [of the Red Cross] because he felt that they would not be able to manage the forty children. I think it was a terrible decision to do that. The Sonnenhof has previously managed other things—for example, sixty children. Why would it not be able to manage these forty children now? We would all have helped. If some of those French children could not have been sent to us here, then some of the other children in the Sonnenhof—the curative education cases—could have been sent here, which would have allowed us to accept the recommendation. I can only suspect that Pache rejected it out of a fear of Bort, because she is always whispering in his ear that the actual mission of the Sonnenhof is the curative education and nothing else. It broke me up inside when I heard that this rejection had been communicated without my knowledge, and the way I see it, what has just happened is connected with this; you have certainly heard by now that Nurse Lissau—Hanna Lissau—has just been deported in France. Pache recommends that we should discuss this with the French Counsel and make clear to them that Hanna Lissau was not an emigrant but rather active in humanitarian work with us, and that we should also stress that even before the war, we were tending to French children both here and in France, and that we now care for war-ravaged French children here in Switzerland. I do not believe that I will get very far with this reasoning, though of course I will try. It would have been very different if I could have said, "We just took on forty children, and the authorities in France should not behave so ungenerously." If I could then have said that we were seeing to it that Hanna Lissau could go to England and that she should be given time to do so, I am all but sure that we could have accomplished something; it seems to me doubtful that such an approach will work now.

Therefore, I am very depressed, and I have the feeling that we are losing ourselves in little personal matters while the larger things are not being grasped. Ever since this thing happened with Pache, I have felt a constant inner weight burdening me—and I did say several times in the past that misfortune awaited us—and so I was not surprised when I received the letter today from Pache with this news [of Lissau's deportation].

Our situation is extremely difficult, even here in Ascona— much more difficult than it was last year.[176]

In spite of all of these burdens, Ita Wegman worked immediately and proactively on behalf of Hanna Lissau, informing her family of the situation, personally contacting the French ambassador in Bern as well as Jules Sauerwein in Paris, the Red Cross, and finally the current Swiss Minister. She also pursued, with great energy and all of the means available to her, the immediate transfer to Switzerland of Vala Nikitina Vachadzé-Bérence, who was just as endangered and had already been imprisoned once, as well as the children being cared for in southern France. But Ita Wegman could do nothing to alter Hanna Lissau's fate. "Perhaps what is now occurring is a kind of Last Judgment," Ita Wegman had written in July 1941, shortly after hearing about the banning of The Christian Community and the arrest of its priesthood.[177] Now she despaired at her own powerlessness, according to Wegman, which resulted more from the failure of her colleagues and anthroposophic friends who lacked the courage to meet the great demands of the future than it did from the urgency of the time and the spiritual *Zeitgeist*. However, in regard to Hanna Lissau, Wegman—who was evidently very clear in the moment about the tragic magnitude of what had occurred—wrote in a letter immediately after learning about her deportation: "I will always hold her in my heart."[178]

"I have my hands full with work"

Ita Wegman, 1942

The Last Three Years: Ita Wegman in Ascona, 1940–1943

In December 1942, Werner Pache visited Ita Wegman in Ascona and had a long conversation with her about the political situation in Europe and what sort of developments could be expected, but also about what she intended to do in the midst of this ever-growing inferno. Afterward, in his diary Pache made note of some of what Wegman said:

> From one terrible perspective, she saw the possible union of a conquered, weakened Germany with an unbroken Russian Bolshevism. That would be a terrible marriage. Lucifer and Ahriman. Spirit is not possible under those circumstances. At best, through something that is both curative education and humanitarian.... Then she would like to go to Germany, completely alone, going from friend to friend and maintaining proper consciousness of the activity of the spiritual world.
>
> Frau Dr. Wegman is completely filled with a sense of this inner mission.[179]

Ita Wegman shared similar thoughts and perspective with Madeleine van Deventer at around the same time:

> Frau Doctor saw herself traveling the world alone—at most accompanied by one other person—visiting friends, traveling from one to the next and whispering in their ears: There is a spiritual world and Rudolf Steiner is active there![180]

3.

"Experience Christ through Community"

Ita Wegman's Spiritual Work in Ascona

> "She spent her days in a harmonious alternation between outer activity and inner study. She was at peace with her surroundings and with the forces of destiny; this gave her the peace needed to immerse herself into the depths of an inner vision of the connections present in life. She strove to take up the whole of Anthroposophy in herself, to work through it inwardly, to allow it to develop anew in her heart. She could then bind this to the inner core of her essential being and carry it over into the spiritual world."
>
> —Margarethe Bockholt[181]

Long before she moved to the Casa Andrea Cristoforo, Ita Wegman had carried the inner longing and desire to work spiritually with a small community of people—"in intimate togetherness with a small circle"[182]—with great and connective continuity, without the interruption of frequent travel, something that had been a part of her life in Arlesheim before the outbreak of World War II.

In the Casa, Wegman held two spiritual-scientific lectures a week on the same days that she had in Arlesheim (Thursday and Sunday) and always before a circle of thirty to thirty-five people—patients and residents of the house, but also friends and interested individuals who came from the nearby surroundings, as well as colleagues from the Motta who traveled there by bicycle. As Ita Wegman said to Hilma Walter, she wanted to "work through all of Anthroposophy and [anthroposophic] medicine once again from the beginning"[183] in Ascona, both for herself and in the sphere of a self-formed spiritual community. This spiritual work was, for Ita Wegman, the actual and unquestionable center of the Casa Andrea Cristoforo: "What connects the people here is anthroposophic work, which can be done well here. I myself can work very well here and can offer a lot."[184] Furthermore, she considered it essential for the further course of world historical development in Germany and Europe: "If spiritual work is not able to be carried out by us in one form or another, it will have a negative effect on Germany's future."[185] It would also be a true preparation for the time after the Great War. In July 1940, Ita Wegman wrote to the pianist Walter Rummel:

> I consider it my task to maintain the continuity of spiritual work and to maintain this continuity everywhere so that the people here will be welcomed once again after peace is reached and the borders are open to everyone once again, for this opening of the borders is something that must occur once peace is reached, or perhaps even before.... This is something for the future that lives very strongly in me and that will certainly be realized one day.[186]

In addition, in a letter written half a year later to the Cologne art dealer Wilhelm Goyert and the German friends in his circle, she wrote, "Tell everyone that I am always occupied inwardly with building something new that must come into being for humanity—something that is impossible without Germany's help; so this group of people must feel that they are part of a community in order to consider themselves members of this constructive work."[187]

After the war, Ita Wegman wanted to travel in many different countries, meeting young people everywhere and sharing Anthroposophy with them in new, distinctly heart-centered ways: "'If this new form is not found,' she said, 'then the war will have been in vain'" (Liane Collot d'Herbois).[188]

―

Many of Wegman's patients in Ascona, as well as many of those who came to her lectures, had until then stood at a distance from Anthroposophy. From the beginning, Ita Wegman's intention had been to be open and welcoming at the Casa, independent from and unencumbered by all of the proceedings in Dornach.[189] Steiner had once warned of the threat of complete public misunderstanding of Anthroposophy, in that it would come to be identified with the problems and the misshapen form of the Anthroposophical Society and its functionaries.[190] Despite the spiritual-epochal activity of the Christmas Conference, this eventually did come to pass, which lay heavy on the soul of a person like Ita Wegman whose thoughts were with all of humanity and who took a very broad view of things. At the beginning of May 1940, she began to establish a free place, dedicated to the possibilities of the future, a Michaelic place where each and every person active in spiritual work who came, whether as patient or guest, was essential: "Everyone who strives is my friend." Whenever, after some period of time there, a patient or convalescent left, Wegman would often send letters after them in which she described her experience of the departure of supportive individuals; she was thankful for the steps forward that she was able to take in her own efforts to gain knowledge of Spiritual

Science: "And it is tremendous how many new perspectives are opened, and with that, I have complete and total proof that this goes hand in hand with the inner development of each individual human being. It is a matter of understanding these things, and if only many people, moved by their own inner development, could understand these things with gratitude, then humanity would be greatly served by it."[191] She was also grateful for the very concrete experience of the spiritual community for which she prepared lessons and in whose attentive presence she established her own work. In a letter from July 1940, she wrote:

> When we come together on Sundays and Thursdays, I miss your presence; particularly on the first Thursday [after your departure], this feeling was very strong. Through your understanding of spiritual matters, you created a beautiful atmosphere for the person who was giving the lecture.[192]

Two years later, she remarked in a letter to a departed couple:

> Yesterday, on Sunday, when I was giving my lecture, I felt that the two of you were not there. It is very strange that one can notice something like the absence of several listeners who participated in the work very intensively in their souls, and I wanted to share that with you.[193]

When an Arlesheim art therapist who had come to the Casa for a long period of recovery traveled back home, Wegman was even clearer with her:

> Your sustaining power belongs with our efforts to attempt to experience the Christ through community. This is the greatest problem that we must solve. And the fact that, in order to bring about this community, it is also necessary for people to distance themselves from it, only to reconnect with it later, seems to me a necessity that might be compared with the fact that people must die and then be reborn.[194]

"Experience Christ through Community"

Casa Andrea Cristoforo

What must be remembered here is that Ita Wegman considered her anthroposophic study evenings and afternoon lectures in the Casa Andrea Cristoforo as an eminent component of her medical-therapeutic efforts. Wegman knew that underneath many life crises, moments of exhaustion, and bodily illnesses lay unresolved spiritual questions, pieces of unexpressed or unresolved life in the spirit, as well as tasks of fate that needed to be recognized or, at the very least, gradually intuited. Carefully, but with a definite eye toward the individual, she lead them to Anthroposophy and to the process of developing as individuals in the spirit sense, never in a missionary-like way, but always with a great and independent gesture, with a sense of earnestness and spiritual dignity. Filled with a great feeling of responsibility for her task, she diligently prepared each of her evenings, which were to have a constructive effect, generating life forces and offering orientation: "This time, it is about starting to talk about what we gradually want to build up in ourselves as we approach one truth after another, that we might be able to hold these powerful images clearly before our eyes." She also wanted to make sure that the patients who left were able to continue their studies and spiritual exercises at home, whenever possible, and she mentioned this clearly in her letters: "It is very important to me that you return to Anthroposophy once again; it is so very important for your work and your health as well."[195] For example, she wrote to an Austrian officer, who had been at the Casa for a long time, shortly after his return home:

> Have you started to read about Anthroposophy? It worries me that you have so little time to work with these spiritual matters, which are so essential and so important for the immediate future. I believe that many demands—spiritual ones—will be placed on Central Europe. There will have to be a great amount of suffering there, but then will come a great unfolding of powers—powers that will save humanity—and we must all be ready for that.[196]

―

Wegman's spiritual activities were intended to prepare the future, establish the groundwork, and foster and strengthen the people—activities she accomplished amid the World War, not in a paradisiacal oasis of time. Ascona and the Casa Andrea Cristoforo, as well as the Motta, did indeed lie far from all of the military fronts, but nevertheless, Ita Wegman sensed in her great, spiritually open soul, which had been highly developed through intensive esoteric schooling, the atmosphere of destructive conflicts and the acts of violence, murder, and death: "Only when the process of initiation is undergone in all its decisive trials is one worthy of being allowed to stand at a distance from this murder that is so dominant on the fronts."[197] Wegman wrested very consciously and purposefully her spiritual-scientific studies and meditative efforts, as well as her lectures themselves, from the demonic powers of evil and death: "Often Frau Dr. Wegman would step into the room with the gravest of expressions; often she would make that hand gesture, so characteristic of her, as though she wanted to brush a spider web away from her face."[198] In the restrained words of Madeleine van Deventer: "With her spirit, she took in the events of the world and was untiringly concerned with seeking ways in which the spiritual could be preserved on Earth."[199]

To that end, from 1940 to 1943, Ita Wegman found herself in inner, spiritual confrontation with various searching spiritual streams that traditionally had their home in the Ascona area;[200] these streams also influenced countless of the guests and patients in Ascona. Wegman once wrote to van Deventer, "We have a strange collection of people here—'Jungian' visitors, as well as various people from last year, such as the mathematics professor, Ostrowski, the chemist from Sandoz, Dr. Stocker, and then various other people from the opposing side. So we have to watch this closely."[201]

Ita Wegman had an ability to differentiate clearly between the "true and false paths of spiritual research."[202] She was a person open to the world and to many things, but she was also an advanced student and colleague of Rudolf Steiner; she knew all about the fatal consequences of false compromises and about the significance of a collapse of original Anthroposophy, and she carried a great number of Steiner's statements and personal remarks on the subject permanently in her heart. Among them were several intimate conversations that she had with him at the end of his life. Regarding all of these questions, Wegman did not conduct many discussions—as had been her approach already in Arlesheim—but rather listened with an open soul and great presence of mind to the frequently distressed people who came to her, after which she would share with them her own thoroughly anthroposophic view and point them clearly toward Rudolf Steiner's life and work. In a letter to van Deventer, written in the summer of 1941, she described the situation in Ascona thus: "I spoke [in the Casa] about the reality of the mass, and Jung is speaking about the symbolism of the mass. Is that not strange? I speak about Gnosticism and Max Pulver does the same, stealing from Dr. Steiner. We are standing in the midst of spiritual battle!"[203]

Liane Collot d'Herbois wrote in her memories of Ascona:

> Frau Dr. Wegman considers it to be one of her primary tasks to fight back against the overwhelming number of apparitions and phantasms that originate in Gondishapur. During the war, she spoke of that often. Then she tended to say as she paced the room: "Fighting phantoms—that is what I am doing!"—and for those she knew well, she would add, "You know that, right?"[204]

—

As had been the case during her years in Arlesheim, the Michaelmas and Christmas festivals were the central spiritual events of the Casa circle. Even in the last years of his life and work—indeed, even during the time when he was sick in bed—Rudolf Steiner shared the deepest insights in the Michael Mystery, its connection with the Christ being, and its significance for the world-historical mission of the anthroposophic movement. Aware of Steiner's detailed remarks on the subject, Wegman tried, beginning in 1924 to 1925, to do work based on this dimension of Anthroposophy.[205] In one of her

Ascona notebooks, she made notes on the inner preparation for Michaelmas:

> In the fall, when the natural world begins to die.
> Before the soul the symbol of the grace. Then the thoughts of Michael, which do not move toward intuition as do the thoughts of Easter, becomes active in people. In the light of fall, an appeal is made to the will; take up those thoughts in yourself, the thoughts that conquer the Ahrimanic powers, the thoughts that make you able to gain spiritual knowledge here on Earth, that you might then conquer the powers of death.
>
> Thoughts of Easter appeal to intuition
> These thoughts of Michael to the powers of will
> The Michaelic thoughts of Michaelmas in the fall as the opposite pole to Easter thoughts
> How does one achieve the strength for proper Michaelic thoughts?
> The divine-spiritual of the higher worlds streams through me
> St. John's Eve summer solstice[206]

As early as the fall of 1940, Wegman wrote in a letter that she understood the Michaelmas festival at the Casa as a "substantiation" of the spiritual work conducted there during the summer, and that she wanted to lead people to the last lecture Rudolf Steiner gave, on September 28, 1924, in all of its greatness and meaning for the future and legacy of the work, "in order to make clear to us what was intended,"[207] but also in light of everything that was happening, the catastrophes and destructions culminating in that moment.

One year later, at Michaelmas in 1941, when Wegman had to be temporarily in Arlesheim and lead the Michaelmas work there, she wrote to Hilma Walter in Ascona:

> One hopes that you were able to have a good Michaelmas there [in the Casa]. It is certainly not easy in these times to carry out in all of its immensity something as deeply spiritual as that which is connected with Michael. It will certainly not be possible for long. First of all, we do not have the strength to do it, and second, there are no people there to receive it. I found it very hard to carry off here in Arlesheim, but in the end we managed.[208]

On the same day, immediately after Michaelmas, she wrote in another letter, this one to Margarethe Bockholt in the Motta:

> Yesterday evening we celebrated the last thing connected with Michael. I found it much, much harder than it had ever been. But in the end, something good managed to break through, and in the same moment, a child was born in the clinic, during the night at two o'clock—so, still half-Michaelic.... All of that gives the clinic a different aura.
>
> I sincerely hope that you were able to carry out these spiritual things in the Casa and the Motta. The times are so incredibly difficult, and most people do not suspect the severity of the attacks by Lucifer and Ahriman, who ensnare the human being in illusion and the propensity for untruthfulness.[209]

Ita Wegman knew well about the things she hinted at in these letters. Connected very deeply herself with the Michael Mystery and having battled and dealt, in the spiritual *Zeitgeist*, in a condensing world ever more occupied by opposing forces, she was now attempting through a renewed and—biographically speaking—final effort to create some free space for spiritual work and to achieve, through these partial breakthroughs, something on behalf of human consciousness as well as for other embattled and endangered beings. To put it in her own Michaelic words: "to see the deeply spiritual through in all of its immensity." Against this backdrop, she approached times like Easter and Michaelmas, but also the Holy Nights with tremendous inner energy, absolute solemnity, and determination. During the period leading up to Christmas 1941 in Arlesheim, a time full of renewed worries and difficulties, she wrote to Madeleine van Deventer in a warning tone:

> It is possible that all of the difficulties now coming toward me will make it impossible to have a strong Christmas, and this absolutely cannot be the case. It cannot be weakened either by lack of money or by sickness. So I ask you then to keep in mind, because it is most certainly the case, that we should expect heavy blows from the opposing side.[210]

A short time later she wrote another advisory letter to van Deventer, this time with a suggestive note in the margin: "I also feel that if I do not lead a strong spiritual Christmas work, it will not have good results."[211] The spiritual Christmas work, according to Wegman in other letters from the same period of time, should be built up "very systematically"[212] and "carried through"[213] in a decidedly spiritual manner. There must be human communities on Earth during these times that succeed absolutely in "connecting deeply with the spiritual,"[214] "allowing the things that the Holy Nights want to give us to flow in, completely objectively,"[215] but also in carrying into the future the spiritual processes enabled by the blessing of these special days and nights: "It is very important to hold together, otherwise every Christmas that succeeded will go up in smoke, if the times that follow it do not bring about any change in people's hearts."[216]

> "She allowed all of Anthroposophy, which was active in her like a living being, to flow anew through her soul." (Madeleine van Deventer)[217]

The Last Three Years: Ita Wegman in Ascona, 1940–1943

Ita Wegman's lectures during the years 1940–1943, which she prepared in her notebooks, encompassed—on the basis of collective work with many of Rudolf Steiner's courses—the evolutionary developments of the cosmos, world and culture, the process of becoming in humanity and the old spiritual high cultures, the mythologies, and the essence of the pre-Christian Mysteries and their cults.[218] But with steadily increasing frequency, they also dealt with—in addition to the Mystery of the progression of the year or the life of the soul after death, as well as a lecture on Christian Rosicrutianism[219] and Rudolf Steiner's life, dying, and death[220]—descriptions of the secrets of this "change of eras" and of esoteric Christianity: the preparation of the incarnation of the Christ, the Christological processes of the baptism in the Jordan, the three years and the Mystery of Golgotha, the three-day "Ascension" of the Christ, the formation of the resurrection body, and the effects of the Christ on the etheric.[221] Already at the center of her first Christmas festival in Ascona, Ita Wegman turned to Rudolf Steiner's lectures on the Gospel of Luke, but also to the course in Karlsruhe, "From Jesus to Christ" lectures, which she spoke of before the Christmas tree lit with candles, the "living red roses" in the Casa Andrea Cristoforo. Something very special lived in and around Ita Wegman during these December days in 1940, a Christmas glow of grace in the midst of the destruction that all those present, including Ita Wegman herself, felt deeply:

> This first wartime Christmas lives in the memory as though we were all protected, together, in a blue grotto with the child of heaven in the middle, radiating light outward to all of us. Outside, the stars shown in gleaming splendor in the black night sky—then reflected again in the lake—no streetlight disturbed the brightness of the stars, which shone brightly because all other illumination was darkened. The deep peace of the Holy Nights washed over us—our consciousness of the

war was there, of course, but it was as though it was very far away. (Erika Müller[222])

During this period of time, we perceived something like a blessing that allowed us, in peace and quiet, to immerse ourselves in spiritual things while the world went up in flames. It is a blessing, but at the same time it is also a great duty that we are able to have this experience in Switzerland. May this not be taken away from humanity! Perhaps many great and beautiful things could still happen in Switzerland. (Ita Wegman[223])

In the period that followed, Ita Wegman penetrated ever further into the inner substance of the Christ processes of the past, present, and future, and she herself, after all of her injuries and difficulties, quite clearly went further through the seven-step path of Christian initiation—"Every person can and should go through these steps at some point"[224]—the individual soul-spiritual stages of which Rudolf Steiner had described in earlier lectures.[225] It led to the formation of new capacities for transformation within her, to powers of love, life, and forgiveness connected with the Mystery of the sacrifice.[226] In Ascona, according to Madeleine van Deventer, Wegman undertook an "inner working through the often painful experiences of her life,"[227] in parallel to the immersion in the essential substance of Anthroposophy and in the transformative and sacrificial paths of the Christ being. As Wegman often said, "The only thing that offers life is reverence for the Mystery of Golgotha."[228]

With the painter Liane Collot d'Herbois, Ita Wegman touched on several of these connections in conversation and gave her Steiner's corresponding lecture presentations to read, with a particular eye toward the Urn Chapel, which was to be painted on the grounds of the Motta. Wegman wanted Collot d'Herbois to paint the Casa stairwell with scenes from Parzival and the walls of the chapel with depictions of the Passion. In a later report, Liane wrote:

> The Way of the Passion was a theme that was very near to her. At the time, it seemed curious that she should be thinking about her death, because she was very well then, full of life and laughter. She explained to me that Rudolf Steiner had told her that, if her ashes were kept after her death, she would be able to work through them in the earthly sphere, not only in the place where they were kept, but all over. That was her reason for having that chapel rebuilt and getting it in order.[229]

The Thursday evening and Sunday morning lectures in the Casa were carried by Ita Wegman's spirituality as it continued to ripen and be expressed in the world, carried by the great transformative powers of her soul, full of the Christ: "To understand the Christ impulse means not merely to strive for perfection, but rather to take up something in oneself that really accords with the word of Paul: not I, but the Christ in me."[230] After Ita Wegman's death, Ludwig Polzer-Hoditz described how one felt "a relationship to the Being of the esoteric ritual" in her proximity.[231] Wegman's audience in the Casa noticed this, in any case, and they were deeply moved by her authentic and deeply experienced words. She began with the words, "On the last night of the year, it is our duty to look back in a comprehensive way at what is happening in the world and at the things that are happening to us and in us. We must stand now as though we were standing before the Judge of the World. The Last Judgment is already beginning for us."[232] Then, when she continued with a description of the Holy Nights and the path of the human soul's development, something irrevocable happened in the hearts of all those present. Something began to move that was connected with the new, with the future that Ita Wegman was striving for on behalf of Anthroposophy—the future she was preparing and living through herself—enabled by particular conditions of her destiny and won through uninterrupted practice and her fight for victory.

It became ever more difficult, if not impossible, for Ita Wegman to carry on doing old things in the old ways. When Madeleine van Deventer and Marianne Bischoff expressed in a letter in December 1940 how much they regretted that, because Wegman was staying in Ascona, no esoteric class lessons were held at Christmastime in Arlesheim, she answered:

> I am very sorry that you were thinking of things this way. Mostly I did not offer so many classes at Christmastime because Christmas should be for everyone, and the classes exclude some people. It would certainly not have worked at all this time, and it generally seems to me as though we should all be even more active inwardly so that the classes become more effective. Something in me expects of everyone who has done the work in the clinic and participated in the classes that they have resurrection thoughts—me most of all. The old repetition of the same things without a dynamic development often has the effect of crippling one. So you should not be sad; it is good for something, perhaps only for me. Therefore, I would like to express my wish that you do not feel resentment toward me when I follow an inner necessity.[233]
>
> Do you really believe that it is absolutely necessary for there to be classes again? It seems to me so antiquated whenever nothing new comes about in people. The classes must be resurrected and taken up in a new way.... I would so like to bring something new—it is alive in me, but it is so difficult when one only hears that they want the classes back again just as they were. However, there must be a process of ripening so that the classes can reach a higher level with people.

I am always working on that, and I have progressed much farther in many things during the Christmas period.[234]

Ita Wegman was not questioning the esoteric class lessons and certainly not the reading of Rudolf Steiner's words ("they may be read *only* aloud,...because in that way, Michaelic words, as Dr. Steiner spoke them, will be given to you again, unaltered"[235]), but she believed that the inner activity of those present should be elevated. "Resurrection thoughts," processes of transformation and ripening, forces of Christ were to move into the people's souls— "me most of all." The advance of Anthroposophy and of esoteric Christianity was never a question of form, but rather of content for Ita Wegman. It was about the inner substance and power of presence in the individual as a precondition of further spiritual happenings, in a social sense as well.[236]

Ita Wegman's lectures, which had in earlier years been infrequent and initially unskilled, ultimately became evidence of her constant and ongoing spiritual-scientific and esoteric work, her occult training, and her ever-deepening growth into the spiritual sphere of the world's foundation. Increasingly, she spoke freely, in a conversational tone, completely confident and individual; she was inwardly active in images and connections indebted to Rudolf Steiner, but was also completely at home in the sphere of her own sense of individuality. She had been awakened to these thoughts with great intensity during the course of her life in the twentieth century. In one of her notebooks, she prepared another New Year's Eve lecture with thoughts of Christ, Michael, the Michael School, and the spiritual tasks of the twentieth century, and wrote:

> Another year has rushed by unnervingly on hurried steps, and suddenly we find ourselves at year's end. This year did not bring with it many beautiful things. We see pain and worry all around us, and some souls would despair at the

darkness that comes toward them. And yet, a small glow, which often works only very weakly but could become a beam of light, lies within each and every soul. We must find it, bind ourselves to it, then conjure before ourselves the image of the group of disciples who were taken up the mountain with Christ and taught by Him how to walk the path of the soul. We belong with them, for we are also beggars of the spirit—some more, some less—we patiently wish to bear the weight of the destiny that is placed upon us and the suffering that comes with it, we wish to overcome anger and fear and go about our work on Earth serenely, which is to say, gently, so that the Earth might be transformed and not left to the wildness of nature or the exploitation of the dominant culture. Just as gentleness must emerge from the anger of the soul, so must the Earth come along in the metamorphosis and, like the soul, be redeemed, for one cannot ascend to heaven without taking along the fruits of the Earth.

Through this the picture is transformed. The archangel Michael stands there instead of Jesus Christ; around him are souls—many, many souls. He has gathered them as his time approached once more, following on the rhythmic return of his regency over the folk-spirits, as the time spirit and leader of all humanity. All of the souls seeking after spirit, souls of dead individuals still waiting in the spiritual world—souls who were ready to come down and take hold of physical bodies on Earth prepared by the stream of heredity—and many angelic and archangelic beings connected with the development of humanity and the Earth—he collected them all around him and taught that an era had dawned on Earth when the old world would fade away and the Christ spirit would continue to stream toward humanity undiminished. In this event, humanity should create the sheaths for Him, that He might gain entry among them.

The souls of the human beings were filled with wonder and awe, and they felt that the forces of wonder and awe were impressed upon their souls, and that this signified a force of attraction for the Christ impulse, the Christ spirit Who again draws near. And now they became conscious of something [else]: the awakening of angelic consciousness in the astral body of the resurrected Jesus of Nazareth, in whom the Christ spirit had always been active until the materialism of human beings on Earth exerted a crippling effect on this consciousness.

The more the souls were filled with wonder, the more complete was this awakening. Then Michael taught the souls the effects that materialism on Earth created in the suprasensory world. Materialism separated souls from one another, did not bring them together; egoism divided the souls. As a result, the effectiveness of the Christ spirit was weakened and dimmed.

An intensive sympathy now took hold in the souls; a feeling for the pain and joy of others found a space. Bridges were built from soul to soul in love and unity. This shone down into the etheric world of the Christ spirit, bringing new life.

Love and empathy must always be present for the Christ to live. Love should not be confused with sexuality; eroticism has nothing to do with love—here, the higher form of love is meant.

Michael then taught that the Christ spirit, His sheath—meaning in the sheath of the Resurrected One—could not accomplish anything, because morality—the Good—had not emanated from human souls. Their hearts were not pure, and so they could not behold God, but God also could not shine into human hearts. The souls that surrounded Michael felt a tremendous sense of responsibility, deeply impressed upon them, which came to manifestation as *conscience*.

Called forth by expressions of conscience through morality, responsibility and goodness, the Christ spirit lives in its third sheath, in the resurrected form-body of Jesus of Nazareth. Just as the Christ spirit worked in the person of Jesus of Nazareth in a way visible to all, so too did it work within the resurrected body in a way visible only to a small circle of people. He vanished before the physical eyes of those not initiated.

After the Mystery of G[olgotha], He was always deeply connected to the Earth and will forever remain connected to it, as well as to human beings.

However, the materialistic sensibility of human beings tarnishes the sheaths of the Christ, such that one could actually speak of a second crucifixion of the Christ in the suprasensory world. Michael is working against this. The teachings on the mountain by Jesus Christ, the teachings to the disciples on how they were to conduct themselves in order to experience the realm of heaven within themselves, is the complement to the teaching of Michael in the suprasensory world; they belong together, the unfolding of the same soul qualities are demanded in each case—the first time, so that the realm of Heaven on Earth could be experienced within each individual; the second time, so that it might not be lost. Between the two stands the wave of materialism, which has for some time threatened all of spirituality.

Michael called forth the sentient soul, the intellectual (or mind) soul.

The Christ says that the thirst for justice will find its satisfaction in the spirit (this is a quality of the sentient soul). Every satiation that is brought about by the spirit calls forth wonder and awe; it is the transformation from low to high, which brings about catharsis; a deep piety arises in the soul. Michael urges us toward this as well, so that the sheath of the astral body may receive the forces of youth. Christ calls up compassion and love, because the highest love and compassion calls forth the greatest unity and bans separation (tenderness and love between "I"-being and "I"-being). These are the forces of the intellectual, mind soul.

Michael calls up the same forces so that the sheath of the etheric body can receive the enlivening forces of the buddhi, which it had lost owing to the wave of materialism. The pure of heart are, will be, called forth by the Christ; they will behold God.

To become pure, one must want this, even if one already wants to be good and moral. These are forces that live in the consciousness soul.

Michael calls forth the same forces in order to bring the sheath of the physical body out of its compaction and lead it to atman. Michael teaches that every seed of spirit, planted at the proper time, has a rhythm of 33 years, during which time it comes to fulfillment. His teachings will be carried forward on Earth. The Spiritual Science of R.[udolf] Steiner appeared 33 y[ears] after the activity of Michael. R.[udolf] S.[teiner] described for the first time in January 1910 (January 5, Stockholm) that a new time, an important time, would come in which many people would develop etheric seeing and would then behold the Christ being in His etheric form. The experience that Paul underwent will be renewed. People will not only experience the Christ impulse within themselves, but will see the Christ being appear beside them in His etheric form, reaching out toward human destinies, offering advice where needed, healing where there is illness.

The fulfillment of this is supposed to take place 33 y.[ears] later, when humanity will be able to develop enough power that the sheath for receiving the Christ spirit will be ready. This will be between 1942 and 1950. Spirit progress began at the end of the Kali-Yuga in 1899, and the date given for the beginning of etheric seeing is 1933. So between 1933 and 1950, important spiritual events are to be expected. It is no wonder then that the world is experiencing such pains and that all of the demons, together with the adversarial powers, are taking up arms in order to keep humanity from progressing peacefully in its evolution. They intend for this event to pass by without human beings giving it much notice.[237]

4

"Why do all of you distance yourselves so from Rudolf Steiner?"

Culmination, Return, and Death

> "It was most certainly difficult for most of them still, but many of them did well and came along. One always gets something out of it. And so I have the feeling that I have completed something here spiritually and find myself once again freer for the work in Arlesheim. That is how it seems to me, but one can never know what the future holds."
>
> (January 13, 1943[238])

At Michaelmas in 1942, Ita Wegman asked her colleagues responsible for the clinic and the Sonnenhof in Arlesheim to come to the Casa for a conversation. As always, she was in regular contact by letter with Madeleine van Deventer, Erich Kirchner and Werner Pache, and now she wanted to discuss with them the further development of the Clinical-Therapeutic Institute after the end of World War II, giving them guidelines and sharing her plans of returning to Arlesheim following the end of the war and, directly connected with this, of immediately starting construction of a hospital, intensifying all of the therapeutic efforts there. This included increasing production of medicine through Hilma Walter and, with that, generally preparing and outfitting the clinic for the coming tasks it would take on in civilization, one of which Wegman understood to be caring for the homeless people fleeing the war-torn areas of Central Europe: "All the details of plans for the future were discussed this fall" (van Deventer).[239]

During these days at the end of September, Wegman held another esoteric class lesson, while all of these gathered friends were present and offered a magnificent and very individual description of Michael, recorded by Madeleine van Deventer:

> The lecture that she gave during those days was the most astounding that I have ever heard from her. She began with the geological epochs that formed the Earth and arrived finally at the activities of the Titans who rule over the laws of the natural world. They could also be called the arbiters of the world's forces; as darkness and light, positive and negative electricity and so on, they each work in pairs on the opposing movements of the animal kingdom on Earth. The lecture contained an abundance of impulses and revealed itself as the product of thorough study. It was in no way a typical Michaelmas lecture.[240]

Nevertheless, Madeleine van Deventer and Erich Kirchner returned to the clinic in Arlesheim with many concerns; in the late fall and winter 1942 the difficulties there escalated once again,[241] particularly in regards to the social life and work of the colleagues there, creating unresolvable situations for the people struggling on behalf of the place and its needs. Even Madeleine van Deventer, after years of fighting, began to despair, despite her choleric, strong-willed, and assertive nature. During November and December, she often turned to Ita Wegman:

> I again requested Dr. Wegman's help. She continues to delay her return. She said to Dr. Bockholt in Ascona: "I myself do not know the solution." A letter came in response to my last

"Why do all of you distance yourselves so from Rudolf Steiner?"

request that contained no answer to my question but revealed the deepest reason for her inner concerns and doubts during these years. The letter began with the words: "Why do all of you distance yourselves so from Rudolf Steiner?"[242]

―

But it was not only the situation in Arlesheim; rather the whole situation in the world that weighed heavily on Ita Wegman in the winter of 1942–43. She still had to fight daily for the right to keep her patients at the Motta, for the permission to stay and to work for her colleagues, for refugees, exiles and the homeless, for each and every person.

Meanwhile, the Great War continued and was reaching a catastrophic scale. While the Allied military prepared to "blanket" bomb large German cities, the National Socialists under Adolf Hitler carried out "total war," as well as the systematic and unthinkable extermination of the Jewish population in the gas chambers of the concentration camps. Ita Wegman did not have adequate information about these plans and the processes that were already under way. However, she felt the immensity of the situation that was arising, sensing and experiencing these catastrophic developments, also on an esoteric level. During these weeks, she shared with Liane Collot d'Herbois that she felt herself "cut off" from the spiritual world.

Nevertheless, Wegman worked with great intensity on the preparations for her last Christmas festival including all of the details of the planned bazaar, for which she energetically ordered (among other things) the printing of a new retelling of the legend of St. Odilia by Nora von Baditz, indicating in various letters seeking support for the effort how much the experience of Christianity on the Odilienberg represents a "source of power for holy love."[243] It was no less a source of power for the intended spiritual work in the Casa itself. Early in 1941, after making a first beginning with it in Arlesheim in 1938, she had spoken about the Revelation of St. John during the Holy Nights, a book that Rudolf Steiner interpreted as early as 1908 as a work with great spiritual-scientific value that had made "the deepest aspects of what we call esoteric Christianity" appear to him—the deepest essence of "Christian initiation."[244] This Christian initiation was and is, according to Steiner, an initiation into the Mysteries of the will and the future; the Revelation of St. John should be a book that "gives impulses for the future, for how to proceed, how to act,"[245] and as such, it should be a kind of training book for the "small ground of people," who, according to Steiner, would rescue the spiritual principles that they had taken up and awoken in themselves from the "general rubble heap" resulting from the "terrible devastation of culture."[246] Ita Wegman had been familiar for many years with the spirituality and images offered in St. John's Apocalypse, as well as with the content of Steiner's lectures in Nuremberg, the earlier remarks in Paris,[247] and the Apocalypse course for priests of The Christian Community, which she had participated in as a member of executive council in September 1924. At the end of her life, however, the depths of Wegman's loving devotion and insight grew remarkably. At Christmas 1941, she had then, for the first time, shared her own experiences and insights in relation to the Apocalypse in the spiritual space of that Casa community, which Wegman, closely following Steiner's words, intended to prepare for the future. Although she wrote to van Deventer in Arlesheim at the end (on January 9, 1942) that the recently completed Christmas work on the Apocalypse had gone "quite well," she added that she probably got the most out of it, "because several things became clear to me that I have been thinking about intensively for a long time."[248] Ita Wegman was dissatisfied with how things had gone and had the impression that, despite a difficult struggle, she had not really "broken through" spiritually.²⁴⁹ And so, during Advent 1942, she shared with the surprised residents and colleagues at the Casa Andrea Cristoforo that she would again be trying to make the Apocalypse the theme that Christmas, "'because we did not totally succeed in grasping the depths of St John's visions,' as she put it."²⁵⁰ In a letter dated December 7, 1942, Wegman wrote, "The work that I would like to undertake [in the Holy Nights] would focus on the Apocalypse, if that were possible; it entirely depends on the people who are there."²⁵¹

Although Ita Wegman then became very ill shortly before the Holy Nights, she began her evening lectures on December 24 after she had been brought the short distance from her house to the Casa by car. In her notebook, she formulated the words with which she intended to open this gathering:

> We have come together, as we do every year at this time, to celebrate a festival of memory. This year did not bring much change; we continue to live in darkness, just as we did last year. It would be a mistake to think that we have gotten any closer to peace. Peace cannot come about through armed victory; peace can only come about through insight and knowledge. It is wrong to think that the activity of Christ is connected with one particular party or nationality. Wherever there is fighting, no realm of peace may arise in which insight and human knowledge are striven for, even if these official sites of peace are called churches and full to the breaking point with people whose souls have been ensnared. The desires of these souls is tied up in egoism and nationality, and this is not what will lead to something new, which humanity so desperately needs—a new orientation in life.
>
> So we must truly be thankful for those sites of peace in which people are striving for insight and knowledge.
>
> And even if the place in which we now find ourselves is quite small in comparison to the larger world—even if it does

not reach out across the Earth yet—everything that has ever grown large began small. When the efforts are true and serious, then in sites like these people will be active in trying ever more to know the true essence of the Jesus Christ—in the past, the present, and the future.[252]

On the following day, Ita Wegman, despite her still weakened state, went to visit and to play in the Motta, as she had during both of the preceding years, and she was very active once again with "her" children.[253]

The Christmas work in the evenings at the Casa Andrea Cristoforo intensified from day to day, from night to night. Ita Wegman spoke about the tree of life, the tree of the knowledge of good and evil, and the tree of prophecy, about St. John and Mary–Sophia, about Ephesus and Patmos: "And it was actually the impulses that he [St. John] carried within himself from the cult of Ephesus—the cult Word—that continued to work on him and prompted him to Patmos in order to perceive the Apocalypse."[254] She also spoke about the approaching catastrophes in both the natural world and civilization and about the workings of the Ahrimanic powers, but also about the future community of Philadelphia, which would emerge from the Great War and carry out healing work.

In his final Apocalypse course for priests of The Christian Community, Rudolf Steiner had shown how the Ahrimanic forces would bring about future disorder in the planetary system and cause great catastrophes; he also pointed out the extent to which only spiritual work and ripening of the human being could work against this reality: "Only the strong spirituality of the human being will be able to counterbalance the disorder that will be brought about."[255] Ita Wegman now spoke out of this spirituality and intention in ever-intensifying evening lectures, completely out of her own seeing soul, open to the spirit and immersed in the substance of the esoteric path that she herself had walked: "It is meaningless to take up the Apocalypse in such a way that one merely comments upon it. It is only meaningful to approach the Apocalypse in such a way that one becomes someone who has personal visions of the Apocalypse, and through this process learns to understand one's own time, that the impulses of that era can become the impulses of one's own actions" (Steiner).[256] By the end of her life, Ita Wegman had undoubtedly developed occult organs for the events and process connected with the Apocalypse; indeed, she had taken up the Apocalypse in her own "I" just as Steiner had described to the priesthood in September 1924: "Such that your "I" becomes the sum of the active forces that are themselves apocalyptic."[257] One of the attendees at Wegman's lectures in Ascona later wrote:

> Then, a great wonder came to pass, intensifying from evening to evening. She spoke freely—the words flowed effortlessly—the powerful images of the Apocalypse were there before her spiritual eyes, and she simply described what she saw. Her gaze was directed into the distance—"it" spoke through her—that is how I see it in my memory. Everything was so boundlessly immense, that in certain moments, a sense of trepidation would grip your heart; the question arose; it is all so unimaginably great, what is to come next?[258]

The shortest but nevertheless quintessential description came from Nora von Baditz: "During the Holy Nights, she [Ita Wegman] spoke about the Revelation of St. John, summarizing all of Anthroposophy in its essence."[259]

―

Immediately after the end of the Holy Nights, Wegman once again dedicated herself to the economic conflicts in Arlesheim

The Last Three Years: Ita Wegman in Ascona, 1940–1943

Ita Wegman, 1942

"Why do all of you distance yourselves so from Rudolf Steiner?"

and Ascona, as well as to the difficult resolution of many other problems, with all of her power and spiritual determination. On January 9, 1943, she wrote the following in a letter after giving a detailed sketch of several oppositions and burdens: "And so the blows are coming in from all sides, as they do every year [after the end of the spiritual work of Christmas], and we will likely have the power to resolve them."

But at the start of February, Ita Wegman recommended to Werner Pache, among other things, that a division for young criminals be established at the Sonnenhof in order to take up a future mission for civilization and strengthen the significance of the place. "It is only meaningful to approach the Apocalypse in such a way that one becomes someone who has personal visions of the Apocalypse, and through this process learns to understand one's own time, that the impulses of that era can become the impulses of one's own actions."

Ita Wegman went into the Christmastime in 1942 with many thoughts and questions about the future, concerns, and considerations; one of her central questions was again about the conditions in Dornach. For seven years, she had distanced herself from the events and constant fulminating debates that happened there; the organization of the executive council as an esoteric board that Rudolf Steiner had founded had been irrevocably and successfully destroyed by 1935 at the latest. All that followed this demonstrated that the world mission of the Anthroposophical Society was not being carried out in any way by the remaining organization. The Dornach Goetheanum stood inactive in the face of a world that was destroying itself, busy with its own internal problems on a war-free island in Switzerland, frequently acting like a "backcountry sect" (Steiner[260]). In Wegman's view, human beings and human civilization, as well as the Earth and the cosmos, needed Anthroposophy more than ever, but nowhere was the official anthroposophic organization taking a large and brave step forward with any sense of perspective. When the young curative educator Helen Eugster informed Ita Wegman in September 1941 of her decision to leave the General Anthroposophical Society, Wegman, who had not considered herself a Society member since 1935,[261] responded with complete understanding: "I have for a long time been of the opinion that it is better to be independent of the Society. It is no longer the time for that. We must attempt to find new forms through which we can live Rudolf Steiner's teachings"[262] (September 9, 1941).

In January 1943, Wegman also responded to Werner Pache's similar decision to leave, though her response was decidedly more restrained: "I was interested to hear that you have left the Anthroposophical Society. I have heard that many young people are doing this. Perhaps the Society should be dissolved."[263] Despite her dissatisfaction with the current form of the Society and its representatives, Ita Wegman still felt the spiritual tie that had once formed through the collective with Rudolf Steiner, and the proceedings in the Dornach Goetheanum continued to be of interest to her after all those years. Ita Wegman knew the undissolvable historical and future-building potency connected with Steiner's central place of work and the school that he had founded, even if the people who were active and operative there at present were behind in understanding their active tasks—or indeed, seemed to have lost all awareness of what those tasks might be. Ita Wegman discussed these matters repeatedly with Liane Collot d'Herbois; in Collot d'Herbois' recollections of this topic, Collot wrote:

> Dr. Wegman saw many connections between the situation in the world and the situation in the [Anthroposophical] Society.

"Why do all of you distance yourselves so from Rudolf Steiner?"

She said to me, "If the three parts of the Society are not able to come together, then this whole war will have been in vain." She foresaw the end of the war and was always inwardly occupied with the question of how this war could be transformed into something constructive. She was of the opinion that if the Society continued to be divided, it would lead to catastrophe. The Goetheanum—the "heart of the Society"— should in her view be seen as a group of people who concern themselves with the spiritual world. When people unite their powers and work together as bearers of spiritual impulses, a harmonizing impulse could be achieved for the whole world.[264] (caption of "Letter from Ita Wegman to Günther Wachsmuth, October 20, 1941)

A few days before the dawn of the Holy Nights in 1942 and Wegman's second Apocalypse work in Ascona, it was Marie Steiner who unexpectedly raised her voice in the pages of the weekly publication *Das Goetheanum*, demanding a fundamental, forward-looking reconciliation of the quarrels in Dornach.[265] In her remarks, she wrote:

> What is...to be done when a Society that has inherited a holy duty on behalf of world history, a Society that has a work to protect and to further without which humanity will surely degenerate, finds itself entangled in problems that it cannot solve? It wants to live up to the duty that it is destined to fulfill, yet it cannot free itself of the restrictive chains and burdens because it lacks the individuals, on whom it depends, able to overcome them. But following blindly solves no problems. What is to be done? The Society must consciously take up the resolution to conquer itself and move beyond these things. Clearly and willfully.
>
> As a Society, we are presented with the question of whether to be or not to be. The catastrophes that have befallen us because of the World War; the barriers between countries, the impoverishment and so on would seem to make

it impossible for us to sustain an external body. But miracles do still happen. They happen when the moral substance is strong enough to justify the miracle. What can we do to rescue our moral substance?

We can forgive! Every person can forgive that which is his to forgive. We can forget that which deserves to be forgotten and not remain stuck on injustices once done to us. We can draw a line under all the old stories that demoralize us; we are in no position to be so demoralized by them, inasmuch as we are young and isolated. We can hold ourselves to this statement: The only thing that is true is that which is productive. We must be able to work together again in harmony, without excluding those to whom we feel antipathy—no one who is true to the effort and to Rudolf Steiner, in order to protect our collaboration; we should not close ourselves off and bar the door to those seeking the spiritual knowledge that only Rudolf Steiner can give them; we should not push away those seeking souls on whose behalf he consciously chose the path of martyrdom; out of love for humanity—for all of this errant humanity. Love, in him, became knowledge—and it can become that for us as well, if we choose that path.

We stand now before the twentieth memorial of that disastrous fire that took from him his earthly life, even though it continued to glow as a sacrificial fire for nearly two years, bestowing upon us an unsuspected spiritual treasure with its flames. Can we not, in the sight of this sacrifice and this death, the guilt for which we all carry, as individuals and as a Society—for he took our karma on himself—can we not forget, forgive and open our doors wide to all those seekers?

It seems to me that this is the only possibility for our purification—as a Society and as individuals. I say this in full awareness of the weight of these words, in awareness of the fact that, by human estimation, I will soon be stepping before Rudolf Steiner's spiritual figure. Let us rescue his work and human culture by conquering ourselves and reconciling to one another by opening our doors wide to all those who seek.²⁶⁶

Ita Wegman was astonished and confused, and despite being considerably shaken inwardly, she was questioning and doubtful of these published words. On January 13, 1943, which was already more than three weeks after Marie Steiner's publication, she wrote to Werner Pache, still moved, troubled, and skeptical:

> It seemed to me, when I read the article by Frau Dr. Steiner, as though she did not write it with an earthly consciousness— she did things without a sense of responsibility for what effect they might have and without any sense of responsibility for what she herself had brought about in earlier times; all of that was missing. It touched me in a strange way. One cannot actually take what she is doing seriously. And I remember that Dr. Steiner always had the same opinion of her, even though some things naturally had to occur through her. Well, we could talk about many things that cannot be put in a letter.²⁶⁷

Despite all of her doubts, Ita Wegman turned Marie Steiner's words over and over in her soul, often on quiet and thoughtful strolls through the Tessin landscape. She contemplated a reply— in spite of the repeated warnings of those surrounding her, which said that Marie Steiner was not thinking of a reconciliation with her, Ita Wegman, but merely had taken a stand against the current conflicts in Dornach itself. Ita Wegman was warned against humiliating herself by over-interpreting that article personally; but she replied harshly:

> You are ruining everything for me with your skepticism. It is not important to me what Frau Dr. Steiner intended in her everyday consciousness. A hand has been extended in her words, and if I do not reach out to grasp it, then I am guilty.²⁶⁸

Rudolf Meyer, a priest of The Christian Community who knew Marie Steiner well and had also corresponded with Wegman for a long time, advised, however, as follows: "If you ask me, then I can only say that I believe she [Marie Steiner] is on some level very *serious* in the intentions of her letter; but I also believe that she is overlooking the deep consequences it would have if others (and also she) were to realize it completely. It could, however, have a significant effect if *you* were to find a way to answer this letter—an answer that really takes seriously the things that are said there." At the same time he described certain past dream-experiences with Marie Steiner from the Holy Nights that moved him deeply: "For she is an unsolvable riddle to me. I had—and have often had—the most wonderful dreams about her during the Holy Nights, in which her being appears to me in such a way that it completely disarms me."[269]

Meyer's carefully thought judgments from the ranks of The Christian Community priesthood, which meant a great deal to her for her whole life,[270] was very significant for Wegman, especially as it was partially based on evaluations that Ita Wegman was familiar with and agreed with, even when it came to the positive qualities of Marie Steiner: "Now and again she [Ita Wegman] would stand in the middle of the street, as though she were somehow able to think better there, and after a while she would lift her gaze to heaven, nod with a quiet smile and say in a quiet voice, 'Yes, that Marie Steiner, *she* is it.' And her voice took on a warm tone when she said this" (Collot d'Herbois).[271] Finally, in the middle of February, Ita Wegman replied—despite everything that Marie Steiner had done to her since 1925—in a genuine act of initial forgiveness, and as such, an act on the path of Christian initiation:

> Your article could be construed in so many ways. I do not allow myself to have a judgment of it. With these lines, I can only hope, quite sincerely, to express that your words made

a deep impression on me—they are so great and full of the future. For that, dear Frau Dr. Steiner, I am grateful.[272]

Six days later, on Sunday, February 21, Ita Wegman embarked on her last journey to Arlesheim. Madeleine van Deventer wrote later about the act of writing this letter and its effect: "It was as though writing that letter made her free for the path into the spiritual world."[273]

Since the beginning of the year, Ita Wegman had been especially worried about Werner Pache's future, but also about Erich Kirchner's, as there was the threat of their being called up for duty in the German army. Although Wegman was firmly of the opinion that Germany should be protected and not fall prey to an unconditional destruction, she pleaded on behalf of Werner Pache, and to a lesser extent on behalf of Erich Kirchner, for a stay in Arlesheim and for an immediate move and transfer of citizenship to Switzerland: "You must take your destiny firmly in hand."[274] On February 9, she wrote to Pache:

> Though I do have the very strong feeling that all forces must now be mobilized for Germany so that it might not have to fall into catastrophe, I also have the strong feeling that we must defend a front that is connected with Germany, and that front is the spiritual work that cannot be allowed to fail, and I have the strong sense that you belong among those whose task it is to maintain that front, and through that work do just as much for Germany as though we are fighting on the eastern and western fronts.[275]

Shortly after this, on the same day she wrote the letter to Marie Steiner, she sent another letter to Werner Pache at the Sonnenhof, calling him energetically to action:

In the end, we do not have much time to lose. At any moment, something might occur that will make the situation worse. Yesterday evening, for example, many planes flew over the local area on the way to Milan, coming so near that the glow of flares could easily be seen. It was an enormous number of them, and it gave the impression of something bringing death.[276]

As early as February 3, Wegman had said that she had a great need "not to delay too long"[277] her trip to Arlesheim; now, on February 20 and 21, she parted very consciously from the people and the surroundings of the Casa[278] and returned to Arlesheim on the eve of her sixty-seventh birthday. Later Nora von Baditz noted the Sunday morning of Wegman's departure from Ascona:

> As I walked through the springtime landscape, I was greatly surprised to perceive a new sort of light above the jagged peaks of the mountains. Still full of this experience, I sat down at the midday table. Frau Dr. Wegman's place across from me was still empty. Suddenly she came and sat down. When I looked, I saw this same fullness of light above her brow. Her look confirmed this experience. It was a process of her conscious expansion into the natural world of the south that she loved so dearly.[279]

On the following Monday morning, under a bright and shining sun, the children of the Sonnenhof brought the first flowers of spring to the wooden house on the day of Ita Wegman's birth, which had long been a major holiday in Arlesheim. Many other people came as well—countless colleagues, friends, patients, and guests who were very moved by Ita Wegman's return, on this day of all days. Ita Wegman, on the other hand, had eluded this practice for years, spending her birthday alone and in hidden quiet. In 1941 at the latest, she longed for something else, and wanted "to

"*Why do all of you distance yourselves so from Rudolf Steiner?*"

disappear in some way."[280] The year before she had tried to do this by fleeing to Zürich, though this had only been somewhat successful and had ended in a premature and involuntary return to the Casa, to the people who, once again, were waiting there for her with gifts, flowers, greetings, and letters.[281] Wegman's path in the twentieth century was unconditionally social, dedicated to people, living, fighting, and often sacrificing herself for them; she could not distance herself from them, and in the core of her being she did not want to. Of course, this was the same core and depths of her being where she realized the possibility of spiritual retreat, her hidden, meditative life, which she maintained daily despite all of the external demands.

On the evening of February 22, 1943, Ita Wegman was finally together with Madeleine van Deventer in the theater and saw the "Magic Island" [Zauberinsel], an operatic adaptation of Shakespeare's *The Tempest*: "With tremendous interest and deep inner joy, Frau Dr. Wegman followed the moving processes of the elemental world and whispered cheerfully during certain scenes, 'All Kamaloka experiences.'"[282]

The negotiations with the immigration authorities in Bern the following day regarding the naturalization of Werner Pache and Erich Kirchner were successful. In the evening, Wegman returned, tired but not dissatisfied, to the clinic in Arlesheim and the wooden house. In Madeleine van Deventer's report about what happened then, it reads:

> Now the impression grew stronger that she was occupied inwardly with very different questions. For immediately upon returning home, she began a unique conversation with several friends, in which she engaged us with an almost Socratic sort of questioning—questions that related to the spiritual relationship of various individuals to Rudolf Steiner. She thoughtfully listened to our opinions and spoke with a deep sense of solemnity about her own convictions.[283]

On Wednesday, Ita Wegman met with many people again and had intense conversations with them, writing letters to Ascona about her experiences in Arlesheim and Bern—to Mien Viehoff and Margarethe Bockholt[284]—thanked people in the Casa for their birthday greetings and gifts: "The change in the scenery was so sudden this time, that it was like being in a dream. In a very short period of time, I had much to experience and to attend to. It was painful for me to have to leave the Casa the day before my birthday and not be able to enjoy everything that had been prepared, but I had no choice."[285] She saw several patients for medical consultation, as she also did on Thursday morning.

Then Wegman fell acutely ill with a high fever and flu-like symptoms. On that Thursday evening, February 25, she reported to Madeleine van Deventer—for the first time from her sickbed—that she had responded to Marie Steiner ten days earlier:

"Why do all of you distance yourselves so from Rudolf Steiner?"

When I...asked her, if she wanted to see Frau Dr. Steiner again and promised to bring her to her sickbed, she answered, bewildered: "Why? The tragedy is over with this life. There is nothing between us now that will stand in the way of future collaborative work with Rudolf Steiner." When I asked her again if, in some corner of her soul, there was a wish to see the original executive council reformed, she answered with great certainty: "No, I would not want to give up this regained freedom." From that point forward, her gaze was directed only toward the future.[286]

Friday morning, the second day of her sickness, Hilma Walter hurried from Ascona to be with her; she, who had once rescued Wegman in 1934 from a severe and nearly fatal sickness, put all of her therapeutic powers to work on a possible recovery, taking over the nighttime watch in Wegman's wooden house. Ita Wegman slept little, and although she had definitely closed the door on all the affairs in Dornach, she spoke in great detail during better hours about the course of the World War, expressed concerns about the possibility of Bolshevism spreading into Western Europe, and followed Mahatma Gandhi's hunger strike in India with great interest. Gandhi had once visited the institute for curative education in Clent, which was supervised jointly by Ita Wegman, who had invited him to the Medical Section in Dornach and Arlesheim, a trip that had unfortunately never proved possible. At the time, Wegman had stressed Gandhi's tremendous historical significance in a letter to Fried Geuter and indicated to him that Rudolf Steiner had once pointed out Gandhi to her as the person who was capable of finding an inner connection to esoteric Christianity and bringing it to India.[287]

Wegman took an objective view of her own sickness, was thankful for all of the therapeutic efforts, but also stressed that their outcome was not yet certain. Ita Wegman already lived in many parts of her consciousness in the spiritual world, which she had known inwardly for some time. "If no spiritual work [on Earth] is possible in the near future, then I will die,"[288] she said in the course of her final days to Madeleine van Deventer, growing progressively less talkative and removing herself step by step from the worrisome conditions of the wartime year 1943,[289] but also from the people that she had *collected* during her lifetime and united in collaborative work.[290] Decades of intensive work under the sign of the actual *Zeitgeist* lay behind her, decades of building up therapeutic and social work through existential dedication and spiritual motivation, among them the blessed years when she worked near and ultimately at the side of Rudolf Steiner, up to the hour of his death.

Ita Wegman died after exactly seven days of illness, at about ten o'clock Thursday morning, March 4.

> She lay there still and peaceful. She expressed no words of advice or wishes for the future. All that was to be said had been said long ago. In the end, death was but a small step for Ita Wegman.
>
> It is not for us to draw any one conclusion from such a life. What we felt was that she was taken over to the other side with love.
>
> From this side, we experienced her serene calm, her complete dedication to the decisions of spiritual powers, and her unbreakable loyalty to Rudolf Steiner. (Madeleine van Deventer[291])

> The day began in bright radiance. An unspeakable magic spread out across the whole of the natural world. It was as though the natural world was celebrating the soul that was parting from it, and then, as though in the growing light of the rising springtime sun, the dear departing soul turned toward us from the spirit in love. A mood of consecration was spread

"*Why do all of you distance yourselves so from Rudolf Steiner?*"

across the land, alongside all this great and human pain. And this mood of consecration could also be perceived in everything as a sustaining force as it now began to carry on Dr. Wegman's great, all-encompassing work. (Hilma Walter[292])

Later, Madeleine van Deventer wrote about the events of the first hours and days after Ita Wegman's death:

> We sat together in Erich Kirchner's work room, which was immediately below the room where she had died in the wooden house. What would happen now? We have to continue working. It will probably be necessary to inform the Goetheanum. Of course.
>
> When I called Albert Steffen during the next few hours and reported on Ita Wegman's passing, he seemed to be very moved. He wanted to know many details about her illness and then asked if it would be alright for him and Dr. Wachsmuth to come. We made arrangements for the following morning. I asked Herr Steffen to take over the communication with the other two members of the executive council.
>
> Dr. Vreede had been in the neighboring room during the last hours before Ita Wegman's death, together with the rest of the doctors and several of the other colleagues who were close to Ita Wegman. She could not and did not want to believe that it was over. When death claimed her, we all called out in the room. Then they all gathered together and spoke the Rosicrucian verse in emotional but spiritually collected voices.
>
> On the same day, we did not accept any other visitors apart from a few sculptors whom we had asked to prepare an impression for a death mask.
>
> Dr. Bockholt, who had to remain in Ascona to attend to the patients there after we had called Dr. Walter, came in the evening, together with some of her friends from there.
>
> The following morning at 10 o'clock, Herr and Frau Steffen and Herr and Frau Wachsmuth came. They remained at her death bed for a long time, where Dr. Walter and

Dr. Bockholt were keeping watch. Much must have been going on in all of their souls. As they were leaving, Albert Steffen asked me for more details about her illness in the front room. He was especially interested when I explained to him that Dr. Wegman herself had spoken of a form of illness that would start to appear frequently in the near future. For many people—as we later learned—these were moments of reflection that were of great significance for their lives from that point on.

On the same day, Jan Stuten visited me. He told me about what an impression the news of Wegman's death had had on Marie Steiner, particularly in connection with the letter that she had received shortly before that. Only now did the full significance of the letter become apparent. Stuten offered the assistance of the Goetheanum for the musical and other artistic arrangements for the cremation ceremony. I had to turn down this offer, because I was inwardly sure that such a ceremony would never have been what Ita Wegman wanted. For her, one could only imagine a very simply ceremony, of the sort that we had held on our own since the separation from the Goetheanum. At the end of the conversation, Stuten asked on behalf of Frau Dr. Steiner whether we would have anything against them holding a memorial service in the Schreinerei, of the sort that Marie Steiner liked to hold there. I answered that of course we could not have anything against this. After all, the Goetheanum had its own, genuine spiritual connection to Ita Wegman. Whether or not I would take part in it, I could not say.

A large wreath came from the Goetheanum with wonderful words on the ribbon that spoke to spiritual reality—something of the sort that referenced the general teachings of Rudolf Steiner.

We had asked Dr. Vreede to speak at the cremation ceremony on March 8. She agreed with an awareness of her duty as a member of the original executive council. We knew that it was very difficult for her—particularly since it was to be expected that Albert Steffen and Günther Wachsmuth, whom she had not seen since 1934, would be present. She spoke wonderfully and did justice to the significance of the moment.

In addition to her, Werner Pache spoke on behalf of her colleagues. The words struggled out of him with noble passion, although he also had to repudiate certain slanders and unjustified assessments of Ita Wegman and her work that had been expressed in past years.

Edmund Pracht contributed the artistic portion of the ceremony. He had composed a very beautiful piece of mourning music that was played by an ensemble of lyres. The actions of The Christian Community were performed by Professor Ernst Fiechter.

In the clinic, we had held a private ceremony on the evening of March 6, at which Dr. Vreede also spoke. That evening, she spoke these words: "Now the decisive spiritual weight of our movement is in the spiritual world."

Madeleine van Deventer also made notes on the essential remarks and sentences of Elisabeth Vreede's memorial speech on March 6, 1943, in the clinic. Van Deventer's fragmentary notes read as follows (with a few cautious grammatical corrections in certain places):

> We are a large, displaced collection, but under other circumstances it would grow much larger. It is already much larger, not here, but in the spiritual world.
>
> The mortal shell is only a small part of what unfolds in the spiritual world. We perceive this as a riddle, but that which is liberated from the bodily is great and very powerful. Puzzling, when we think about short periods of illness. Much must be newly prepared, much in the spiritual world. Perhaps this process is necessary for great tasks in the world.
>
> The soul of Ita Wegman was connected with cosmic thinking. Not a thinking with the intellect, but rather a thinking that was connected with all of humanity. This

came about because her soul had guarded itself against moving into intellectualism too early, for she was born on Java, and this allowed her to develop the inner heart forces. Karma intended that she quickly find her teacher at the beginning of the century; from this time onward, there was a spiritual connection between the two of them. Then she decided on studying medicine. During the period of time that Dr. Steiner was holding his lecture cycle, "World, Earth, Human," in Stuttgart, Ita Wegman was a student in Zürich. Then came the time when destiny sent Dr. Steiner to Switzerland, and the group continued to travel from Zürich. In the meantime, she had completed her exams. Then she had a practice in Zürich, in which she was already active in realizing the spiritual within the physical. When she founded the anthroposophic clinic in Arlesheim, Dr. Steiner turned to her and said, "It would be good to work together with you." Dr. Wegman found joy in this clinic, despite how difficult it was to be practically active. It was a happy opening for her, and that also pleased Dr. Steiner. This inner collaboration, for which there was a spiritual understanding, was what Dr. Steiner had liked about Dr. Wegman. Dr. Steiner said to her, "You are a person with whom one can communicate as a human being; otherwise one would suffocate."

In Ita Wegman, a lot came forward out of a rich past, and at the same time, something was there that belonged to the future. The spiritual was her directive, and she acted accordingly; this is foreign to many people nowadays.

Everything I had said so far is concerned with the soul. Behind that, the spirit stands as an image, and it will be much more difficult to speak of that. There, one steps onto a territory where tragedy is to be found....

When Dr. Steiner was very ill, she asked him, "What will happen, when you are no longer there?" Dr. Steiner answered, "At that point, karma will prevail." Ita Wegman's soul was not rattled by this karma—she, whom Dr. Steiner called his friend and with whom he was connected. Both of them were connected with Michael and the battle that Michael led—she was an example for that battle. She demonstrated what it is like when a human soul is already fully living in the spirit. This force in the spirit held its ground against the onslaught of opposing forces. It is difficult to understand what it means when a soul like Rudolf Steiner's transitions into the spiritual world and other souls remain here; but here, one can come to understand that.

For us, the decisive spiritual weight of our movement has now moved over into the spiritual world. This is important to consider; it means that it is important to consider that necessary decisions will be made in the spiritual realm. One might ask, "How is it to continue?" Indeed, the decisive spiritual weight of our movement has moved over into the spiritual world, but we feel that we must continue to carry her and we must muster the courage to do so through that which is not in the spiritual world and gives us power, the power to build, which has now been liberated. What is connected with this life [Ita Wegman's] and death? The fact that we see that a soul is truly lived and led by the spirit.

"We are born from the spirit"—this means that the human body comes from the spirit;

"In Christ we die"—which means that the soul meets Christ in death, and everything we can experience on Earth is an experience that comes through the Holy Spirit—"that we may be awakened in the spirit."

―

The urn with Ita Wegman's ashes was moved to Ascona and found its home after Liane Collot d'Herbois completed her work on the frescos in the chapel on the Motta estate: "She said that Rudolf Steiner had told her that she would be able to continue her work in the earthly sphere after death, so long as her ashes were housed and protected—and she would not only be active in the place where her ashes were housed, but rather everywhere. This is why she wanted to renovate and decorate the chapel."

> Spirit triumphant
> flame through our feeble,
> hesitant souls.
> Burn up all egoism,
> ignite compassion,
> that selflessness
> river of life for humanity
> shall be the source spring
> for being reborn in the spirit.
> —Rudolf Steiner

Notes

1 Ita Wegman's notebook. Unpublished. Ita Wegman Archive, Arlesheim. All of the other Ita Wegman notebooks, correspondences, and manuscripts, as well as unpublished manuscripts about Wegman that are cited here can be found in the same archive (Pfeffinger Weg 1A, CH-4144 Arlesheim).
2 Letter from Ita Wegman to Sheila Hirst, Ascona, Feb. 22, 1941 (original in English).
3 Liane Collot d'Herbois, "Ita Wegman," in *Ita Wegmans Erdenwirken aus heutiger Sicht* (Considering Ita Wegman's Earthly Work Today), edited by Andreas Grunelius (Arlesheim, 1976), 15.
4 Letter from Ita Wegman to Madeleine van Deventer, Ascona, Jan. 9, 1942.
5 Letter from Ita Wegman to Werner Pache, Ascona, Mar. 24, 1942.
6 Nora von Baditz, *Die drei Jahre* (The Three Years). Unpublished, handwritten manuscript (1957).
7 Hilma Walter, "Der Lebensgang von Ita Wegman" ("The Life of Ita Wegman"), in *Erinnerungen an Ita Wegman* (Memories of Ita Wegman), edited by the Klinisch-Therapeutisches Institut, Arlesheim, 1945, 16.
8 Madeleine van Deventer, *Autoreferat zu Vorträgen über Ita Wegman zum 100. Geburtstag 1976 in verschiendenen Städten* (Report on the lectures about Ita Wegman on her hundredth birthday, 1976, in various cities), 13.
9 See Emanuel Zeylmans van Emmichoven, *Wer war Ita Wegman. Eine Dokumentation* (Dornach, 2000); in English, *Who Was Ita Wegman: A Documentary;* vol. 1, tr. D. Winter; vols. 2 and 3, tr. M. Barton (Mercury Press, 1995, 2005).
10 See Zeylmans, vol. 2, 230–237.
11 Rudolf Steiner, *Geisteswissenschaftliche Erläuterungen zu Goethes Faust*, CW 272, vol. 1 (in English: *Anthroposophy in the Light of Goethe's Faust*. Great Barrington, MA: SteinerBooks, 2013), 99.
12 Rudolf Steiner, *Vorträge und Kurse über christlich-religiöses Wirken. Band V. Apokalypse und Priesterwirken*, CW 346, 17 (in

English: *The Book of Revelation: And the Work of the Priest.* London: Rudolf Steiner Press, 1998).

13   Ita Wegman, cited in Liane Collot d'Herbois, "'Im Tun neigen sich die Götter.' Persönliche Erinnerungen an Ita Wegman" ("'The gods bend low in action.' Personal memories of Ita Wegman"), in *Mitteilungen aus der anthroposophischen Arbeit in Deutschland,* Heft 171 (Reports on Anthroposophical Work in Germany, vol. 171) (Johanni, 1990), 33.

14   Letter from Ita Wegman to Werner Pache, Ascona, Jan. 13, 1941.

15   Rudolf Steiner, *Anthroposophische Menschenerkenntnis und Medizin,* CW 319 (Dornach, 1982), 29 (in English: *The Healing Process: Spirit, Nature & Our Bodies.* Great Barrington, MA: SteinerBooks, 2010).

16   Ita Wegman, "Das Krankenlager, die letzten Tage und Stunden Rudolf Steiner's" ("The sickbed: Rudolf Steiner's final days and hours"), in *Was in der anthroposophischen Gesellschaft vorgeht: Nachrichten für ihre Mitglieder,* no. 16 (What is happening in the Anthroposophical Society: News for its Members) (Apr. 19, 1925), 63. Reprinted in *An die Freunde. Aufsätze und Berichte aus den Jahren 1925–1927* (To Friends: Essays and Reports from 1925–1927) (Arlesheim, 1986), 10.

17   Letter from Ita Wegman to Erich Kirchner, Ascona, July 24, 1940.

18   Letter from Ita Wegman to Edmund Pracht, Ascona, Aug. 16, 1940.

19   Madeleine van Deventer, *Zur Zeit des Zweiten Weltkrieges* (The Time of the Second World War). Unpublished, undated manuscript.

20   During his course on the Apocalypse in Sept. 1924, Rudolf Steiner indicated that the outbreak of World War I had been connected with a dampening of certain key individuals' consciousness with the lack of a certain clear and conscious waking state that made it possible for demonic beings to become active. On Sept. 12, 1924, Steiner said, "You will never be wrong to say that the roughly 40 people who are the cause of the outbreak of this war had, in the moment when the war broke out, a certain dampened state of consciousness. This dampened consciousness is always the way that Ahrimanic powers are allowed to enter" (Rudolf Steiner, *Vorträge und Kurse über christlich-religiöses Wirken. Band V. Apokalypse und Priesterwirken,* CW 346 [Dornach, 1995], 123 [*The Book of Revelation: And the Work of the Priest.* London: Rudolf Steiner Press, 1998)]). Ita Wegman's almost desperate, but ultimately successful effort to maintain her consciousness in spite of the acute pain shortly after breaking her arm should be seen against this backdrop.

21 Letter from Ita Wegman to Gerhard Schumacher, Riehen, Sept. 9, 1939. Following the lines cited here, Wegman went on to say, "But I believe that one must also learn to do this and must properly resolve the task that is presented by such a situation."
22 Letter from Ita Wegman to Siegfried Palmer, Riehen, Sept. 9, 1939.
23 Letter from Ita Wegman to Gertrud and Wilhelm Goyert, Arlesheim, Sept. 29, 1939. Ten days earlier, Ita Wegman had written to Willem Zeylmans in Holland: "It was indeed a peculiar experience to have to suffer this tremendous pain and to feel what countless people are currently undergoing in far worse ways. These are terrible times indeed" (Arlesheim, Sept. 19, 1939). As one begins to sense the immense, world-historical accountability that was active within Ita Wegman, one also begins to gather some impression of the direction that her thoughts understandably took during the days of Sept. 1939 and also of the terrible burden she felt: "I have had an extraordinary amount of pain and must always return in my thoughts to the unspeakable suffering that humanity is experiencing, for such pain is being felt every day and every hour by thousands upon thousands of people. This is no ordinary thing" (To Nora von Baditz, Sept. 19, 1939).
24 See also Peter Selg, «*Ich bin für Fortschreiten*». *Ita Wegman und die Medizinische Sektion* (Dornach, 2002), 153 (in English: *I Am For Going Ahead: Ita Wegman's Work for the Social Ideals of Anthroposophy*. Great Barrington, MA: SteinerBooks 2012).
25 Letter from Ita Wegman to Hilma Walter, Riehen, Sept. 16, 1939.
26 Wegman wrote to Hilma Walter about this in the letter cited here: "I am very moved by all of the demonstrations of friendship and love. I also heard about the chivalric adventure of Dr. Behre and Frau Stein who lost their way while picking the cyclamen (which are now smelling marvelous and brought me so much joy) and had to spend the night in the woods. It sounds so fantastical that now, after the fact, when we know that all is well, one can laugh about it heartily, which does my soul good."
27 Ita Wegman began renting the Casa Andrea Cristoforo on June 1, 1936, and several weeks later received a license to use the house as a recovery home with 12 beds and shortly thereafter she purchased the facility. This was during a year which followed her expulsion from Dornach and the dramatic developments in Germany: "We are indeed sitting in a very dangerous corner, and I have a great responsibility for the patients and the children at the Sonnenhof who are entrusted to my care" (to Nurse Alma Ganz, Mar. 18, 1936). Wegman was working intensively to anchor the

anthroposophic medicine movement internationally—"... Difficult times lie ahead. But we still have much to do in the world, and we are losing so much time in waiting. I would like to bring about a great intensification of our work" (to Wilhelm Goyert, Feb. 12, 1936)—not least through the successful startup in Paris (rue de l'Assomption) and trips to Iceland, Norway and Sweden, which were meant to strengthen initiatives for curative education there through an "extension of the Sonnenhof" (letter to Bernard Lievegoed, Oct. 8, 1936). After Tessin, Wegman had been keeping an eye out for many years, and already in 1926, when the Arlesheim clinic was being rebuilt, she had rented a house on the Lake of Lugano for several years. In the early summer of 1936, she expressed extreme happiness about the expansions that were finally completed, and her own recovery from a flu on site at the end of June: "I experienced just how unusually healing the climate is there and how lovely it is to be there" (to Wilhelm Goyert, July 3, 1936). She turned over the economic management of the house to Anni Viehoff, established a library, among other things, and sent children there from the Sonnenhof, as well as Liane Collot d'Herbois and her friend Yvonne, for recovery. In numerous letters written as early as 1936, Wegman drew her successful Ascona establishment's attention to the great future significance of this building and its surroundings, and shortly before Christmas she wrote to Nora von Baditz who was already at the Casa: "It is very important to live into the house properly, so that we have a refuge in the South from the difficult times to come" (Dec. 22, 1936). In the ensuing years, Wegman tried many times to entrust the future leadership of the house to successful anthroposophic medical colleagues such as the Dutch physician Rudersdorff and later Gerhard Schumacher from Berlin, who after meeting Hilma Walter at the end of 1938 took over the primary care of the children at the Motta. During this time, up to May 1940, the organization and development of the locale, however, did not meet Wegman's expectations and hopes.

28 For the history and development of "the Motta Farm," see the report by Barbara Schaeffer, "Die Anfänge der 'Motta Farm'" ("The beginning of 'the Motta Farm'"), in *50 Jahre Ita Wegman Fonds für soziale und therapeutische Hilfstätigkeiten* (50 Years of the Ita Wegman Fund for Social and Therapeutic Aid), (Ostern, 1993), 38. In it Schaeffer says the following about Ita Wegman's purchase of the house and the first years there, up to 1940: "Its once prosperous owner, Herr Doman, had fallen on hard times and wanted to auction off the Motta Farm; Herr Pache heard about

this and reported it to Ita Wegman. So she was able to purchase the Motta cheaply. The estate consisted of three large and two small houses on two hectares of land, some of it sloping and some of it terraced. It had been cultivated biodynamically and was planted with beautiful fruit and vegetables as well as a variety of flowers and bushes.... Herr Doman had built the houses as vacation homes, and several children and friends in need of soul care were still there. In the beginning, for a period of time, people in need of recovery time and guests came, and a course for doctors was held there. Herr and Frau Berger [from the Sonnenhof] saw to the house and garden. Then in 1938, Heinrich Händler came with a pupil as the first curative educator, and others followed him, for the Motta offered them more opportunities for activities than the small compound at the Sonnenhof" (ibid., 38). In a letter from Jan. 1937, Ita Wegman had already spoken about starting a little garden in Brissago and taking children there, hence the apparent purchase in 1936 of the estate and the houses, as well as the Casa Andrea Cristoforo. According to Ilona Schubert, Wegman bought the Casa and the Motta at the same time; Werner Pache had noted in his diary that he saw both of the estates himself for the first time on Mar. 25, 1936. In the summer of 1937, the group of children from the curative educational initiative in Paris under the leadership of Vala Nikitina Vachadzé-Bérence came to the Motta as guests, as did several children from the Sonnenhof.

29 "It is so important to have these little centers all over, and by that I do mean internationally. During this crazy time in which everything is tending toward autocracy, the cooperation of people from many different nations is enormously powerful" (letter from Ita Wegman to Nora von Baditz, Riehen, Sept. 19, 1939).

30 When Mien Viehoff, a very close colleague for many years and in many ways Ita Wegman's "right hand," asked Wegman in October for permission to leave the Casa where Viehoff worked in order to go to Paris for a while to see friends and take a small vacation, Wegman made the seriousness of the situation quite clear to her, writing, "I find it quite understandable that you would like to go to Paris to see the city again and to visit your old friends, but you must also be quite clear, dear Mien, about the fact that we cannot free up any money for your sojourn. You also must be quite clear about the fact that the only way we can avoid bankruptcy is through the most serious efforts of all our colleagues and through sacrifices, whether in wages, interest, etc. If we were to go bankrupt, which is very, very possible, then of course all of the past, present and future

work that we do will be swept away, and this is indeed—as you must well understand—the tendency of the forces of opposition. Indeed, the whole war is a war against allowing the spirit to penetrate the non-spirit, and you must also realize that the non-spirit has taken all manner of forms, all over the world. However hard it might be not to have your friends by your side and not to be able to help them, you must always ask yourself, 'Where is fate demanding my contribution?' What we are doing is a work that Rudolf Steiner introduced into the world, and we expect that it will greatly benefit humanity. I have been placed into the battle with the demons by destiny, and I will likely have to fight against them; but woe, if I were to lose or to waver in this battle, for much would collapse without me" (Oct. 24, 1939).

31 In a letter from Wegman to Hilma Walter written on Nov. 1, 1939: "There is no bad weather here now—indeed, it is even sunny—and so far nothing has gone wrong for me here, making it not altogether bad to be here, and indeed, it is necessary for me to be here, because we have to make some sweeping changes. Fifteen people have already been given notice [at the clinic and at the Sonnenhof] and half of them will be gone today. You can understand what this means, and also that everything has to be carried out with a positive attitude. Contracting is much, much more complicated than expanding, and I am happy to hear that things are going well in Ascona and Brissago; this lessens my concerns considerably."

32 In spring 1934, during the culmination of the discussions in Dornach, Ita Wegman was severely ill, and several months later, once she had recovered, she took a trip to Palestine with some friends: "a trip that Rudolf Steiner had actually wanted to take with me." (See Peter Selg, *Geistiger Widerstand und Überwindung. Ita Wegman 1933–1935*. Dornach, 2005; in English: *Spiritual Resistance and Overcoming. Ita Wegman 1933–1935*. SteinerBooks, 2014.) Wegman deeply internalized the country of Israel, admittedly experiencing, according to her later descriptions, much of the old Jewish desert and Judaea aspects of Palestine, interrupted by occasional rain showers and a particular scent that it brought with it, "as though incense were burning and the first seeds were being planted." After her return, she wrote the following to Hilma Walter: "This experience was remarkably important for me and made me conscious of the fact that this is indeed holy ground—this Palestinian soil—where Christ walked" (Nov. 22, 1934). Together with her companions in Palestine, she studied Rudolf Steiner's lectures on the Fifth Gospel (*The Fifth Gospel: From the Akashic Record*. London:

Rudolf Steiner Press, 1988, CW 148), followed by the *Bausteine zu einer Erkenntnis des Mysteriums von Golgotha* (*Cosmic and Human Metamorphosis*. Great Barrington, MA: SteinerBooks, 2012, CW 175) as the time of her long-delayed return approached. During that return, she stopped for a time at both Capri and Rome where she occupied herself with a detailed study of the spread of early Christianity. Deeply moved but simultaneously involved in a series of decisive and major changes, Wegman sent various letters to friends in November and December after her arrival in Arlesheim, in which she began to describe and came to express her changed inner attitude toward the proceedings in Dornach and also her newly found intentions for work. She wrote three letters on December 17, 1934, and said to Walter Johannes Stein, "I now have the strong feeling that my sphere of activity here in Arlesheim must become much more intensive. I must already take up the fight against the demons that are here and protect at least a little piece of Dr. Steiner's work, as he intended it to be carried out, so that the connection with his intentions is not broken"; to Eleanor Merry: "It is absolutely essential that here in Arlesheim there be a place where Rudolf Steiner can continue to work as he intended to do, so that his intentions can be continued here in us. This is indeed a task for which I must continue living"; and to Jules Sauerwein: "They are still fighting in Dornach, but I am no longer concerned with any of that. Fighting and battling in the physical world is a *maya* for me. Spiritually, it all looks quite different, and I hold to this spirit and direct my life toward it, in true connection with Rudolf Steiner. Christianity has not been understood for a long time. You really become aware of this when you are there in Palestine and see that nothing is left of what happened there, no understanding; the Christianity that spread out from Rome also was not practiced in the spirit of Jesus Christ. Thus, we cannot expect the anthroposophists who hear about esoteric Christianity for the first time to have the power and courage to live with this esoteric Christianity, which is deeply connected with Anthroposophy. We can actually consider the external strife and conflict with this in mind, because the souls are unsatisfied with themselves, and they express this by being dissatisfied with others and fighting with them, rather than battling with themselves. It is always possible to make a stand for Anthroposophy and Rudolf Steiner, even in external life—one does not need to walk beside these anthroposophists. Although we have it very hard here, I also feel that a lot of help is streaming down to us from the spiritual world. It is with this hope that I move into the time of Christmas." Ita Wegman had experienced a deeply affecting spiritual perception during the closing days of her nearly fatal illness (in March 1934), about which she wrote the following words to Maria Röschl on Feb. 22, 1935: "I am not expected in the spiritual world. A demand was made [upon me] to do something yet on Earth during an encounter that I had with Rudolf Steiner, at which the Christ being was also present. From that moment forward, I found that I had the strength to take my recovery fully into my own hands." This and the experience in Palestine strongly determined the course of Wegman's life, at whose center she now placed the emergent Christianity and the project of making medicine Christian. Her great Christmas study work at the Clinic in Arlesheim must be seen against this backdrop; that work was first begun on Dec. 24, 1934, under the Christmas tree decorated by candles and roses and lasted through the thirteen holy nights and was repeated yearly, with each year being dedicated to a different Steiner lecture cycle on the Gospels. In a notebook for the speech on Dec. 24, 1934, Wegman prepared the following words: "When I speak these words to you now, I would hope that you take from them that we are now standing at a new beginning. We must experience the Christmas time as full of spirit, must connect intensively with Rudolf Steiner's spiritual bequest and allow it to live anew in our hearts, must try to understand what he intended, must experience anew everything that happened at Christmas and create a synthesis of those experiences—the Mystery secrets from North and South, from East and West. With this, we will experience Anthroposophy anew as something that illuminates our hearts. Let us form an association of people who sincerely want this and who take up this work consciously. May the fruits of that be good! May the spiritual world hear us, hear this plea that I am now speaking on this consecrated night, and take up our efforts in grace, cloaking us with the light of their wisdom. May we succeed in gathering the foundation stones of this work, in erecting the edifice of this work that will grow better and more intensive every year as our powers grow. If we strive to undertake this consciously, we will form a voluntary and unofficial association."

33 "Frau Dr. Wegman speaks: Survived the year. At the start, as has often been the case, it looked worrisome. It brought us the start of the war. One had to assume that peaceful work was definitively over. But this was not the case. She herself had an accident. (She turns now to her colleagues.) She thought it was over as well. 'One always thinks that the things one has established oneself cannot be

carried out by others.' She thought it was time for her to go. But lo and behold—the work continued. Her colleagues were able to maintain it and bring it forward. Now she has been lifted out of it and is freed up for other tasks. Now her colleagues can simply take up help and the advice that she has to offer because she is connected with the work. This is the relationship they have now. The proceedings continue: A note regarding the eightfold path and the corresponding exercise from *How to Know Higher Worlds*. The etheric Christ. Alexander's deep inner longing to search for Paradise. A harrowing feeling as Frau Dr. Wegman speaks about what she carries in herself that goes beyond Alexander (the fact that she does carry this in herself can clearly be seen). (She has come to realize inwardly that the errors of this great tragedy of the Anthroposophical Society, insofar as they have reached her and us, lie in an unwarranted penetration of the Alexander being and spirit.)" Werner Pache, *Diary*, Dec. 31, 1934. Thomas Meyer made a machine transcript of this diary, which can be found in the Ita Wegman Archive. Thomas Meyer published some selections from Werner Pache's diary in his 1991 study, «Vom Fortwirken der Weihnachtstagung: Werner Pache und Ita Wegman» (On the continuing effects of the Christmas Conference: Werner Pache and Ita Wegman), in *Zur anthroposophischen Heilpädagogik und Sozialtherapie* (On anthroposophic curative education and social therapy), vol. 4 (1991), 20–43.

34 Pache, *Diary*.

35 From the undated notebook entries of Ita Wegman. Missing sections of sentences are filled in here, as they are in the following transcriptions from her notebook, though the way she split her lines has been preserved.

36 Wegman wrote about this on Jan. 8 to her colleague Gerhard Schumacher, who was working at the time at the Motta, attending to the children's medical needs: "At the end of the week, patients will be coming to Ascona, as well as children who can possibly be sent later to Brissago, but must remain at least temporarily in the Casa with their mother. Dr. Walter will be departing at the end of the week, as will I, several days later, if I am able to sort out everything with the insurance."

37 Letter from Ita Wegman to Mien Vienhoff, Arlesheim, Sept. 25, 1939.

38 Letter from Ita Wegman to Willem Zeylmans van Emmichoven, Arlesheim, Sept. 19, 1939.

39 Letter from Ita Wegman to F. M. Rummel, Arlesheim, Jan. 19, 1940.
40 Letter from Ita Wegman to Leslie McMichael, Arlesheim, Jan. 27, 1940.
41 In the middle of Oct. 1939, Wegman had already hinted at this in a letter to Hilma Walter: "I am very concerned about the medical work, about the work in general. Only now in the last weeks have I been able to do more spiritual work; before that I was suffering greatly from the effects of the shock and the constant pain in my arm" (Oct. 16, 1939).
42 Julie Wallerstein, *Einige persönliche Erinnerungen an Frau Dr. Wegman aus den Jahren 1933–1943* (A Few Personal Memories of Frau Dr. Wegman from the Years 1933–1943) (Hefte des Ita Wegman-Fonds für soziale und therapeutische Hilfstätigkeiten: Arlesheim, 1982), 13.
43 Pache, *Diary*, entry dated Mar. 4, 1930, in Brissago, exactly three years before Wegman's death. In a further note appended to the same entry, Werner Pache records the content of a conversation that he had with Ita Wegman a few days after the cremation, about Leopold Sparr's destiny, and this offers some hint of the spiritual manner in which Ita Wegman approached these events: "Upon entering his room after his death, without having collected herself, she suddenly had a very strong impression: *Chartres*. It was just as clear as the impression she had in Frau Hemsoth's room after her death: *Constantinople*. When I spoke of my impression, as he lay in state, and also of Sparr's life in Paris and the fact that there is still a person who continued to play a role in Sparr's life up to the end, Denise—whom I would like to get to know—said to Frau Dr. Wegman that Sparr must have lived a signification incarnation in Paris. She alluded to *Abelard and Heloise*. She thought, in Paris, in the *post-Chartres period*, a transitional roll. His suffering—together with the hardships of many anthroposophists with 'relationships'—is perhaps connected with the morals practiced and propagated by the Church. Not *marriage*, which tends too much toward the earthly, but rather relationships. What should be done in spiritual commemoration of Sparr? A "lecture" would not really be so appropriate, at least not as the main thing? Frau Dr. Wegman: Pose questions to the spiritual world (thereby involving Sparr) about the true form of European relationships. For example, Dr. Steiner said that the 1914–1918 wartime association on Earth between France and Russia was a war in the spiritual world between hardened local and softer local [hardened Western and softer Eastern?] etheric

bodies. Is that still the case, or is there actually much more now? The East, with its marriage of Ahriman and Lucifer evidenced by Bolshevism, wants to spread into the West. The West, including Germany, must erect a barrier against it, but in a different way. Pose this question to the spiritual world and commemorate Sparr in this way. Because he shed everything connected with old karma through his sickness; he dealt with it fully, and was likely able to transition directly into the spiritual world."

44 Letter from Ita Wegman to Liane Collot d'Herbois, Arlesheim, Feb. 14, 1940 (original in English).

45 Letter from Ita Wegman to Erich Kirchner, Ascona, Dec. 3, 1939. It was not until thirteen days after Kolisko's death—evidently, after a long period of reflection—that Ita Wegman sent the following letter to Lilly Kolisko in London (original in English):

Ascona, Dec. 12, 1939
Dear Frau Kolisko,
I was deeply stirred by the news of Dr. Kolisko's death and now as I gradually hear from another how it took place I must write you. Such a death is in keeping with his great personality so tragic —as was his whole life—that of a great individuality who did not find the place to live on Earth as he needed. Once Rudolf Steiner said to me that his life now was a preparation for the next, so he will not have long to wait for that one in which he can more fully develop. So we think of him, dear Frau Kolisko, who has gone before preparing the way for us. I do hope the show has not been too severe for you.

It is good that Genie [the daughter of Lilly and Eugen Kolisko] is with you. I hear her first words were, when she heard the news, to go as quickly as possible to London to be with you.

With my deep sympathy and greetings
Yours sincerely
Ita Wegman

At the end of Dec. 1939, Eberhard Schickler requested that Ita Wegman write an obituary for Eugen Kolisko and she agreed: "In response to your question about whether I would write down my memories of our friend Eugen, I would answer by saying that I would be glad to do it as soon as I am back in Ascona" (Arlesheim, Dec. 28, 1939). She did so in March and April of 1940, and it first appeared in the summer of 1940 in the collection edited by Eberhard Schickler, Julia Mellinger, and Jürgen von Grone: *Eugen Kolisko. Bilder aus seinem Leben und Wirken* (Eugen Kolisko:

Pictures from his Life and Work). Ita Wegman received the volume from Stuttgart at the Casa during the beginning of September and was very moved by it, both by the expression of Kolisko's life and work that it contained, and also by all of the friends who contributed, to whom she felt very closely connected: "I would like to send my love to everyone who has written so beautifully. I have been able to connect with everything again in a very living way, which is a very beautiful thing.... Tell all of our friends that I think of them with love. We all feel a great longing to see all of our friends again; hopefully that will happen again before too long" (letter to Eberhard Schickler, Sept. 9, 1940).

46   Letter from Ita Wegman to Hilma Walter, Arlesheim, Mar. 27, 1940.
47   See Pache, *Diary.*
48   Ita Wegman, *Notizbucheintragung* (notebook entry). Undated, Ostern, 1940).
49   For example, she wrote the following in a letter to Walter from Mar. 21: "My question then, which you should perhaps discuss with Annie [Viehoff], is whether it wouldn't be appropriate to purchase here certain things that are too expensive in Ascona, for example coffee and a few other things, and send them along with Frau Pfersich's furniture, which is being sent from here. How much does rice cost? It also seemed to me that the quality of rice in Ascona was not as good as what we have here. Also, you should check to see that melted butter (which is much cheaper) is being used; you can buy it at Migros. And instead of olive oil, we could be using amphora oil."
50   Letter from Ita Wegman to Hilma Walter, Arlesheim, May 4, 1940.
51   See Selg, *I Am For Going Ahead* (p. 153 in the German edition).
52   "Would it not be possible for you and me to live apart from the house with someone who could see to a few things for us, that we might do this work, and for me to ask one of the doctors here to be at the Casa during that period of time? I see this as the only way in which we could work in peace and quiet. Whatever we work up could then be typed by Miss Gilson, if it is far enough along for that. Otherwise, I would even try to take along Frau Koch. Then it would be a work that did us both good. We could go walking, too, which is important.... Think about all of this carefully. I have already received some money, not yet the whole insurance sum, but some daily allowance, and I think that there is no better use for it than to enable us to do this medical work in freedom" (May 4, 1940). Two days later, Wegman wrote in a different letter to Mien Viehoff in Ascona that she and Walter had to be "completely freed

Notes

up" for "medical work" in the near future, and that as a result the Casa would be left to Margarethe Bockholt or Margarata Stavenhaben while she and Hilma Walter would live separately from the others, and added, "which is not to say that we do not want to help, but rather that we need that much time to work undisturbed." As a way of explaining the reasons behind these plans in at least a rudimentary way, Wegman wrote in one sentence that this was a work that she was "spiritually obligated to do" (May 6, 1940).

53   Letter from Ita Wegman to Hilma Walter, Arlesheim, May 4, 1940.
54   Letter from Ita Wegman to Hilma Walter, Arlesheim, Apr. 21, 1940.
55   Letter from Ita Wegman to Betty Aetherly, Ascona, Aug. 31, 1940 (original in English).
56   Letter from Ita Wegman to Walter Johannes Stein, Arlesheim, Sept. 22, 1939. In the second week of October, Wegman wrote to Frida Knauer, a caretaker of the children in Brissago who had sent a package with things the children had made at the Motta to Riehen shortly after her arrival in Tessin: "I hope that you have beautiful weather and take good care of the Motta Farm. It is a comfort to me to know that you are all in Brissago, in a good climate and in conditions that will continue to be sustainable in the future. Although I hope that the war will not continue, we cannot say anything about the future just now. For the time being, it is all quite black. So take care of yourself in Brissago. Help each other when one or another of you gets impatient or longs for the Sonnenhof. Make a new, little Sonnenhof in the south, and I am sure you will succeed at it" (Oct. 11, 1939).
57   "When the workers from the Sonnenhof stepped onto the SBB train platform in Basel with the children, Frau Dr. Wegman was already waiting there with her patients for the southbound train" (M. Scherz, "Frau Dr. Wegman im Jahre 1939" ["Dr. Wegman in the Year 1939"], in *Hefte des Ita Wegman-Fonds für soziale und therapeutische Hilfstätigkeiten*, Michaeli: 1988: 11).
58   Letter from Ita Wegman to Alexander Leroi, Ascona, May 17, 1940.
59   Letter from Ita Wegman to Gertrud Spörri, Ascona, Oct. 22, 1942. Gertrud Spörri (1894–1968) was *Ur-Priesterin* (original female priest) and *Titular Oberlenkerin* (titular bishop or coordinator) of The Christian Community, which she left in 1933 under tragic circumstances, and beginning in 1939, she was active in the International Committee of the Red Cross. In Oct. 1942, Ita Wegman turned to Spörri, whom she had known since the founding of The

Christian Community, for help through the Red Cross in reaching Hanna Lissau, who had been deported and was later murdered by the National Socialists: "In addition to what Herr Pache told you about her, I would like to add that I would be very glad and very grateful to you if you were able to help this child, who is so brave, self-sacrificing and gifted in curative education, through some sort of connection with the Red Cross that might allow her to get to Switzerland. I do not know what sort of possibilities exist, but I know that this poor woman is certainly in grave danger right now" (Oct. 22, 1942). Toward the end of this letter, Wegman went on to say, "How much I would have liked to speak with you again, Fräulein Spörri, and heard about what you have been doing! How wonderful that you have ended up working with the Red Cross! One can do so much good there; it is actually the most important task for Switzerland right now."

60 Rudolf Steiner also spoke many times about the special situation and opportunities in Switzerland due to its particular and exemplary ability to appreciate the tasks of the future (see also the collection of texts and the overview by Hans Hasler, *Rudolf Steiner über die Schweiz* [Rudolf Steiner on Switzerland], Dornach, 1988), particularly in regards to the Threefold Social Order: "Switzerland is particularly called to this, and I would say that the angels of the whole world are looking to Switzerland to see if things happen right here—Switzerland in particular is called to this because it has had only a cultural and an economic state and is completely new to the idea of forming a legal state, which it cannot do independent of cultural and spiritual life" (Oct. 14, 1921, cited in Hasler: 59). Steiner expressed his deep sorrow in various lectures about the many possibilities that the Swiss populace and the anthroposophists living there did not see and take up, particularly during the period of Europe's collapse: "I can only imagine...what it might have meant if the Swiss populace had, in 1914, taken up the great, internationally significant task that is before them" (Sept. 6, 1920, cited in Hasler, 46). However, he continued to hold on to the various options still available there, and even in Mar. 1924, said the following to the General Assembly of the Anthroposophical Society: "We may be allowed to say that as part of the collective events of world history, namely those world events that have a spiritual character, a very significant karmic task has fallen to Switzerland. And anthroposophists should always remain conscious of these sorts of karmic tasks.... I have often said that Switzerland could be a kind of fulcrum for the present circumstances in the world, not only in

external, economic ways, but also (if it could only decide to do so) in regards to spiritual matters. It is really a matter of willing it, and anthroposophists need first and foremost—and please forgive the tautology—they need the will to will this" (Mar.16, 1924, cited in Hasler, 73).

61 As regards this matter, one might look—in addition to Emanuel Zeylmans' illuminating work on the spiritual context for Wegman's decision to open the clinic in Arlesheim and to work in close proximity to Rudolf Steiner—to the complementary account by Madeleine van Deventer, according to which Marie von Sivers had confided to Ita Wegman in an early conversation in Berlin "a statement made by Rudolf Steiner, *namely that in the future, Switzerland would be the only country in which one could expect a certain degree of independence in medical work*" (Madeleine van Deventer. *Autoreferat zu Vorträgen über Ita Wegman zum 100. Geburtstag 1976 in verschiendenen Städten* [Report on the lectures about Ita Wegman on her hundredth birthday, 1976, in various cities]; emphasis by Peter Selg).

62 Letter from Ita Wegman to Ludwig Noll, Zürich, Apr. 5, 1920. A facsimile of the letter can be found in Selg, *I Am For Going Ahead*, 2012.

63 According to a handwritten note by Erich Kirchner, Wegman wrote this testamentary directive right before departing for Ascona and gave it to Else Koch, her longstanding secretary who had worked for her since 1924.

64 Ita Wegman Archive. Excerpts of this were published in Zeylmans, vol. 2 (p. 299).

65 Letter from Ita Wegman to Madeleine van Deventer, Ascona, July 26, 1940.

66 Letter from Ita Wegman to Nurse Heta Ross, Arlesheim, Nov. 4, 1936.

67 In a different letter to Hans Kühn, who had written to her in early summer 1940 with a Threefold Social Order appeal asking for support in Switzerland, Ita Wegman said the following about Ernst Marti: "He [Marti] will be the one who is most likely to be able to do something for the Threefold Social Order in Switzerland. If he manages not to get too involved in his own practice; health insurances practices are not really something that is needed anymore, particularly when there are more important things to be done. But, like all of the Swiss, he has his own ideas" (Ascona, July 3, 1940). Just two and a half weeks later, on July 20, Ernst Marti, stuck in his own concerns, withdrew his own surety for the Arlesheim

Clinic, in response to which Wegman wrote him a long letter that began with the following sentences: "Of course, I assume that you find yourself in a difficult position, or otherwise you would not have done this at this moment, because you can certainly imagine that we will not only be in a difficult position as a result, but the work itself will be endangered. It will be quite clear to you that this work is not connected with me alone, and so this does not do harm only to me. It will also deal a harmful blow to your work and to everything in Switzerland related to our medicine. In these times it is very difficult to find other people who can take over this surety, and there will be almost no possibilities of making arrangements with the bank. I will, of course, do everything that I can so that you are freed from the concerns that you speak of" (Ascona, July 23, 1940). A day later, Wegman once again wrote very clearly about this to her colleague Erich Kirchner, and said in this letter, "I have written to Dr. Marti; somebody should perhaps speak somewhat forcefully with him still. It goes without saying that the Swiss should help, that spiritual life should be borne along together. Why is it always foreigners who do it? How does he think about all of this? The Swiss have not supported my work—at least the Swiss anthroposophists have not, though the authorities have been much more understanding. Steffen, Boos, Englert, Kaelin, and now Dr. Marti, have all actually broken down my work, each of them in his own way, consciously and unconsciously. Now I ask myself whether I should let myself continue to be battered—isn't it time for me to free myself from working with these people, indeed from working in Switzerland at all? I don't yet know how I am supposed to do that" (Ascona, July 24, 1940). In addition to all of the positive things that he saw there (see note 57), Rudolf Steiner also pointed out certain hindrances in many people in Switzerland that prevented them from being able to or wanting to take up energetically and with initiative great and overwhelming tasks, disregarding their own self-interests and personal preferences. Ita Wegman described this quite clearly in the following description, which does not pertain *so* directly to Werner Kaelin or Ernst Marti: "This is the way of things; when you try to make someone in Switzerland warm to the things that are so bitterly needed in the world nowadays, you often fall into despair, because it does not actually pertain to him directly, because your words just kind of bounce back, because he does not actually have his heart in it. It is simply distasteful to him to be of any interest, and he has too little experience with these things for him to be sympathetic to them. He wants to have his peace and quiet. But he also wants to be Swiss. That means that if, for example, all of the various cries for progress resound across the border with tones of 'freedom' and 'democracy,' then because people in Switzerland have called themselves democratic for centuries, they cannot very well say that they do not support democracy! In other words, you really have the feeling that people in Switzerland have a well-developed connection between the right and left ears, such that everything that goes in one side goes out the other without touching upon their understanding or their heart" (Oct. 14, 1921, cited in Hasler, 56).

68 Letter from Ita Wegman to Ernst Marti, Arlesheim, Jan. 10, 1939.
69 Madeleine van Deventer: *Zur Zeit des Zweiten Weltkrieges* (during World War II).
70 "Once, when I was coming into Ascona from Paris, Ita Wegman approached me in a very excited state. She could hardly wait to tell me about a new plan that she had. She had gotten an offer to come to Vancouver, where someone wanted to build a large clinic for her. She was very happy about this and had already decided to go to Canada. And she would have gone, too, if the war had not broken out" (Liane Collot d'Herbois: "'Jeder, der strebt, ist mein Freund.' Persönliche Erinnergunen an Ita Wegman" ["Everyone who strives is my friend." Personal Remembrances of Ita Wegman]. In *Mitteilungen aus der anthroposophischen Arbeit in Deutschland* [Records of anthroposophic work in Germany], vol. 172, Johanni, 1990, 110).
71 Madeleine van Deventer: *Zur Zeit des Zweiten Weltkrieges* (during World War II).
72 Letter from Ita Wegman to Werner Pache, Ascona, Sept. 2, 1940.
73 Letter from Ita Wegman to Erich Kirchner, Ascona, July 6, 1940.
74 Letter from Ita Wegman to Erich Kirchner, Ascona, Aug. 26, 1940.
75 Letter from Ita Wegman to Erich Kirchner, Ascona, Aug. 29, 1940.
76 Letter from Ita Wegman to Madeleine van Deventer, Ascona, Sept. 2, 1940; for more on Ita Wegman's fight with the *demons*, see Emanuel Zeylmans van Emmichoven, *Wer war Ita Wegman. Eine Dokumentation*, vol. 1, pp. 189, 320, and 349 in the German edition (in English: *Who was Ita Wegman?* Mercury Press, 1995).
77 See also Selg, *I Am For Going Ahead*, pp. 88 and 129 in the German edition.
78 Letter from Ita Wegman to Hilma Walter, Arlesheim, Sept. 15, 1940.
79 Letter from Ita Wegman to Anni Ruhtenberg, Ascona, Oct. 7, 1940.

The Last Three Years: Ita Wegman in Ascona, 1940–1943

80   Letter from Ita Wegman to Gerda Strauch, Arlesheim, Sept. 20, 1940. In another letter from Nov. 16, Wegman writes, "For Christmas, I will like to go to Arlesheim, since I was here for Michaelmas" (to Gabrielle Boëthius).
81   Letter from Ita Wegman to Madeleine van Deventer, Ascona, Dec. 2, 1940.
82   Letter from Ita Wegman to Werner Pache, Ascona, Dec. 23, 1940.
83   Letter from Ita Wegman to Madeleine van Deventer, Ascona, Dec. 22, 1940.
84   Letter from Ita Wegman to Erich Kirchner, Ascona, Dec. 26, 1940.
85   Letter from Ita Wegman to Werner Pache, Ascona, Jan. 15, 1941.
86   Letter from Ita Wegman to Nurse Johanna Dost, Ascona, Dec. 23, 1941.
87   Letter from Ita Wegman to Madeleine van Deventer, Ascona, Dec. 23, 1942.
88   Letter from Ita Wegman to Nurse Nel Hogeweg, Ascona, Feb. 28, 1941.
89   Letter from Ita Wegman to Nurse Johanna Dost, Ascona, Feb. 10, 1941.
90   Ita Wegman had the ability to help mediate social crises from a distance, leading obdurate and privately prejudiced individuals back toward the greater whole: "I take up no party affiliations, rather I have only the whole in mind, and this greater portion cannot move forward when people are fighting and misunderstanding one another, but experience has taught us that all misunderstandings and difficult exchanges can be overcome when one keeps one's eye on the greater whole" (to Nurse Wilma Kröncke, Ascona, June 7, 1941). She reminded them of their personal responsibility while also creating openings during escalating exchanges for all aspects of each person's destiny to find expression: "Now, it is generally the case in life that you cannot always make everything as clean and neat as you might a house or a room or a craft project; in human exchange there is also a portion that remains unresolved, because there is karma between the two individuals, and karma relationships are extremely complicated, particularly when there are many people involved. I would advise all of you not to get too hung up on particular events, but rather move past them and sometimes things resolve themselves" (to Marianne Bischoff, Feb. 25, 1942).
91   Letter from Ita Wegman to Madeleine van Deventer, Ascona, May 22, 1941.
92   Letter from Ita Wegman to Madeleine van Deventer, Ascona, June 26, 1940.

Notes

93 Letter from Ita Wegman to Madeleine van Deventer, Ascona, July 22, 1940.

94 Letter from Ita Wegman to Werner Pache, Ascona, Dec. 13, 1941.

95 Letter from Ita Wegman to Madeleine van Deventer, Ascona, July 22, 1940.

96 Because of the need to reduce the size of the clinic, Wegman laid off particularly people from the administrative and economic branches during the spring of 1940: "The only solution is to make Arlesheim as small as possible, so that the expenses there are not large and the clinics' debts can gradually be paid down. This is *one* solution. The second, if it is possible, is to try to bring Arlesheim back to life by taking in new patients and so on. Before we can arrive at the second, we perhaps have to go through the first. If the people do not want to leave, then the only option is that they work for one or two months without pay. If so much depends on the continued life of Arlesheim, then sacrifices will have to be made" (to Erich Kirchner, July 2, 1940). At this time, she also intended to part ways with one of the two business directors, or "administrators," as Wegman put it—either Erich Kirchner or Ulrich Rudolph: "It is a luxury to have two business directors for our institution. One of the two will have to step down. If cost-cutting measures are to be undertaken, then everything must be considered.... Now, there is no rush there, but I do intend it" (to Madeleine van Deventer, June 23, 1940). She was also of the opinion that a disproportionately high number of doctors worked in the clinic: "There is always this excess in the positions of higher responsibility, and a lack of people who really do the work properly" (to Werner Pache, May 22, 1940). Wegman did follow through on her intention to reduce the number of business manager positions, and communicated directly to Erich Kirchner in the summer of 1942: "Further costs will have to be cut in the positions that you and Rudolph hold, for the clinic cannot support two administrators; the two of you should discuss this with one another, since it would be possible either to reduce the salary of both positions or cut one of them altogether" (June 2, 1942).

97 After a visit from Erich Kirchner and Werner Pache in Ascona, Wegman wrote very directly to van Deventer: "Kirchner and Pache have left again. Two strange figures—Pache as cold and hard as a diamond—and it was only on the last evening that we—Pache and I—could have a friendly conversation; Kirchner is simply too much in love with himself—unhappy here, unhappy in Arlesheim, because there is nothing there that nourishes his own self-love. What is to come of all of this? No activity in thinking, no activity

in feeling—just carrying on stubbornly, completely wrapped up in himself" (Aug.17, 1940).

98   Letter from Ita Wegman to Erich Kirchner, Ascona, June 4, 1940. The passage cited here was merely in regards to the repairs of the defective clinic automobile: "I was very astonished to hear the news that the Ford is broken. How is that possible? Who was the last person to drive the car before it stopped working? Who is responsible for the car? People cannot simply go driving around in it without somebody being responsible for it, and when it breaks, then the clinic, which is to say—I—have to see that it is fixed." But its significance was far greater, not to mention the fact that the Clinical-Therapeutic Institute had been for many years part of an association for which Wegman served on the board. She identified herself with the clinic, as she wrote to Erich Kirchner on Aug. 26, 1940, for "though it may be an association, it is my and Dr. Steiner's creation" (ibid.).

99   Letter from Ita Wegman to Erich Kirchner, Ascona, Aug. 23, 1941.
100 Letter from Ita Wegman to Erich Kirchner, Ascona, Nov. 3, 1941.
101 Letter from Ita Wegman to Wilhelm Goyert, Ascona, Jan. 17, 1941.
102 "First [meaning during the period of time when these gatherings were first introduced] she would communicate the word of Rudolf Steiner, reading lectures of his and seeking to deepen the listeners' experience in conversations and through her own explanations. Later, she transitioned into speaking freely about what she had gained and experienced through Anthroposophy" (Margarethe Bockholt, "Das Jahr 1924" [The Year 1924], in *Erinnerungen an Ita Wegman* [Memories of Ita Wegman], published by the Clinical-Therapeutic Institute of Arlesheim (Arlesheim, 1945, p. 44 in the German edition).

103 Letter from Ita Wegman to Werner Pache, Ascona, Mar. 24, 1942. On the same day, Ita Wegman wrote extensively to Erich Kirchner about this topic, saying (among other things): "I do not want to have even more demands placed on me by the Sonnenhof than the ones I am dealing with currently, and things must be kept together until the moment comes when I can take over everything again myself." The "demands" she mentions refer particularly to the doctor Julia Bort's work at the Sonnenhof, which Wegman found unauthorized, socially problematic, and out of step with the overall spiritual intentions of Arlesheim, despite Bort's medical qualifications. Although Wegman had already tried to correct and to limit these failings on Bort's part, and to that end had made efforts to place Hilma Walter at her side (see Selg, p. 153), she had never

succeeded in halting the trend that was developing at Arlesheim in connection with Julia Bort. In a letter to Madeleine van Deventer about her departure to Ascona, Ita Wegman even wrote, in Apr., 1941: "The Goetheanum and Dr. Bort have made it very difficult for me to return to Arlesheim" (Apr. 16, 1941).

104 See also the remarks and letter passages in Selg, p. 106. In regards to a conversation at the Sonnenhof intended to make the medical and curative education initiatives completely Wegman's responsibility again, Werner Pache noted on Aug. 7, 1942: "With the presence of Dr. Bockholt here during the last two weeks, we spoke about several things in connection with the letter from Dr. Wegman [from July 25, 1942, see Selg, p. 106], in which she rejected the weekend plans for Sept. and Oct., referring to the demands placed on her by Ascona currently and by her inclination to start something in Zurich (see below), but also 'because in the future, everything that is to be done in connection with curative education should be initiated and directed by her.' In regards to this, Dr. Bort mentioned Dr. Steiner's last words to Ita Wegman. He must have indicated to her that she would be forsaken by all—or at least by very many people—but not by him."

105 Selg, p. 47.

106 Letter from Ita Wegman to Alexander Leroi, Ascona, Nov. 9, 1942.

107 Madeleine van Deventer, *Zur Zeit des Zweiten Weltkrieges* (The Time of World War II).

108 Letter from Ita Wegman to Madeleine van Deventer, Ascona, Aug. 31, 1940. Wegman also spoke about the elemental spirits' "demand" for a Christian Christmas in a letter to her colleagues in Arlesheim dated Dec. 22, 1940: "I always had the feeling that it was necessary for me to spend Christmas and the Thirteen Holy Nights here in southern Switzerland, celebrating it as we always did. The natural world here is so, I would say, pagan, that one has the feeling the elemental spirits are practically demanding this." For more on the principle significance of this task, see also Rudolf Steiner's remarks from June 11, 1922, in Vienna: "Anthroposophy as striving after the Christianizing of the world," collected in CW 211 (*The Sun Mystery and the Mystery of Death and Resurrection*. Great Barrington, MA: SteinerBooks, 2006) and the remarks collected in CW 26 (*Anthroposophical Leading Thoughts: Anthroposophy as a Path of Knowledge*. London: Rudolf Steiner Press, 1973).

109 Letter from Ita Wegman to Margarete Link, Ascona, May 24, 1941.

110   Letter from Ita Wegman to Alexander Leroi, Ascona, May 19, 1940. In contrast to van Deventer's later account: "The recovery [from the accident in 1939] was very slow and she never again regained all the strength she once had" (van Deventer, p. 1 in the German edition). Wegman wrote in one letter to Alexander Leroi's mother, Juliette Leroi (May 24, 1941): "I am stronger than I ever was," and spoke in other letters as well to the same effect. Indeed, she declared that she "became much healthier...than I ever was before," the next year to Wilma Kröncke (June 19, 1942). She wrote in somewhat more detail—although still only hinting at the key event—in another letter: "Now, as summer approaches, I am so happy here in Tessin with this wonderful view of the blue mountains, the heavens and the water; standing on my balcony, connecting with and enjoying this view for an hour or so has a therapeutic effect on me, because all of my concerns and day-to-day worries disappear. As soon as the war is over, I will be taking a large, all-encompassing journey" (to Baron Hugo von Tinty, Apr. 20, 1942).

111   Letter from Ita Wegman to Jules Sauerwein, Ascona, Aug. 18, 1942.

112   Letter from Ita Wegman to Irene Bergsma O'Brien, Ascona, July 1, 1940.

113   Wegman dealt very consciously and purposefully with these geological aspects of the "geographical medicine" that she intended to create (see also Emanuel Zeylmans' book, volume 2, p. 132 in the German edition), particularly in regards to the mutual development of Arlesheim and Ascona as therapeutic centers. As she described in a letter dated Jan. 1942, the work could be very well completed "between" the two healing centers, "because we the opposition of the siliceous ground here to the chalk in the north is very powerful; and once you have been here for a longer period of time, then you find the chalk very pleasant. So here we have two therapeutic factors connected with one another that, if one allows them to have the proper effect, produce positive results" (Ascona, Jan. 20, 1942, to M. Hoogewerff).

114   Letter from Ita Wegman to Helen Eugster, Ascona, Dec. 20, 1940.

115   Rudolf Steiner, *Das esoterische Christentum und die geistige Führung des Menschen*, CW 130 (*Esoteric Christianity: And the Mission of Christian Rosenkreutz*. London: Rudolf Steiner Press, 2005).

116   In his Locarno lecture on Sept. 19, 1911, Steiner said, among other things: "The transition into the twentieth century is significant for the whole of cultural evolution because of what is flowing from

the East into the West and intermingling with the life there, the result of which is what can be drawn from an experience of the natural world and taken up as something invigorating for the deepest aspects of our soul lives. Those whose spirits are awake will be able to see new beings present in the processes of the natural world. Though people who are not yet clairvoyant, despite their sorrow at the relentless death they see, will experience ever more a sense of refreshment in the natural world, those who have awakened clairvoyant powers will see new elemental beings emerging from the dying natural world. Although the great transformations occurring at the transit into the twentieth century will be little seen in the purely physical world, souls that are open to the spiritual world will sense, 'The times are changing, and we as human beings have the duty of preparing knowledge of the spirit. It will be ever more important to observe such things and carry them in our consciousness. It is dependent upon the will of the human either to take these things up, for the salvation of humanity, or to simply let them pass by, to the detriment of humanity.' There is an intimation of something else in this; here at the transition into the twentieth century, a wholly new empire of natural beings is being born that emanates from the natural world as a new font for the spirit—something that human beings can both see and experience," CW 130, 30 (*Esoteric Christianity: And the Mission of Christian Rosenkreutz*. London: Rudolf Steiner Press, 2005); for more on the pre-history of Steiner's two lectures in Lugano and Locarno, see Nik Fiechter, *Über die Entstehung und Entwicklung anthroposophischer Tätigkeiten in Lugano. Eine Zusammenschau mit geschichtlichen Ereignissen im Tessin* [On the origin and development of anthroposophic activity in Lugano: a synopsis with reference to historical events in Tessin], unpublished manuscript (1988). On Steiner's lecture in Locarno and its significance for Ita Wegman, Nik Fiechter once wrote in a letter: "Rudolf Steiner spoke prophetically in his lecture on Sept. 19, 1911, of the forces that are active here in Tessin. Dr. Wegman was among those who took these up in a particularly strong way, and if you keep Dr. Wegman in mind when you read this passage, you get a picture of her that I find particularly fitting" (letter to Emanuel Zeylmans van Emmichoven, Feb. 5, 1982). According to Ilona Schubert (*Die Casa di Cura—Casa Andrea Cristoforo Ascona*, in *Ita Wegman-Fonds für soziale und therapeutische Hilfstätigkeiten* [Michaeli, 1981]), Rudolf Steiner spoke directly with Ita Wegman, who already had intended to set up a "branch" in the south by the time she was making the first plans for a clinic in

Dornach/Arlesheim (1920), about the need for a recovery home in Tessin "and pointed out to her Locarno or the neighboring area, such as Ascona. He said that the gentle southern air and the magic of the landscape would have a calming, healing effect. Especially the Isole di Brissago would be of great significance. He explained that in times gone by, there had been a Mystery site there—a Druid temple" (p. 14 in the German edition). Steiner himself, according to Schubert (citing other sources), visited Druid stones and tombs during his stay in Locarno and reported about them later to Wegman.

117 A small trace of Wegman's studies and experiences with this theme can be found in one of her notebooks from the Casa, in which Ita Wegman wrote down her lecture manuscript for June 30, 1941, which said early on, "I would also like to try to describe to you the impressions that I had both on the far side and this of the Gotthard—how people are reacting to the [war] events there and here. North of the Gotthard, you find that people still have a bit of the West in them; in the south, they still have a bit of the East. Here you find offshoots of Eastern sensibilities; on the far side of the Gotthard you find offshoots of the Western sensibilities. The Gotthard forms the border. In earlier times, the crusaders felt this as well—the ones who came from Western and Central Europe, as soon as they crossed the Gotthard, felt that things were already difficult, as though they could sense the beginnings of the East that they were pressing on toward."

118 Letter from Ita Wegman to A. Simons, Ascona, June 11, 1940.

119 Letter from Ita Wegman to Ludwig Engel, Arlesheim, Oct. 4, 1939.

120 Nora von Baditz, "Ascona," in *Erinnerungen an Ita Wegman* (Memories of Ita Wegman), edited and distributed by the Klinisch-Therapeutisces Institut, Arlesheim, 65.

121 Letter from Ita Wegman to Nora von Baditz, Arlesheim, Oct. 17, 1939.

122 Madeleine van Deventer began an essay of thoughts on Ita Wegman once with the words: "Ita Wegman on the crest of the wave of an era in which even souls were to be abolished. But her existence was a living protest against this abolishment. All of her soul capacities were in harmony and were strongly developed. Her consequently living thinking penetrated the problems of spiritual and practical life. Her feeling, which embraced all of humanity, had a warmth and intensity that one almost never sees anymore, and her will was forceful. There were no barriers to the realization of an initiative that she considered right. In personal conversations with her, you would often hear the words, 'There is nothing worse than the death

of the soul'" ("Ita Wegman," in *Hefte des Ita Wegman-Fonds für soziale und therapeutische Hilstätigkeiten*, [1976], 3).

123 After the baptism of a child, for example, Wegman wrote the following supportive and orienting lines to the mother: "We can be thankful for the courage of every soul that has bravely decided to come down and participate in the chaos of the physical world, because the younger generation will bring about much that will better the world. It is up to parents and friends to welcome these young souls openly and give them every opportunity to be properly brought up and to have the right soul attitude" (letter to Gertrud Schaub, Ascona, Dec. 10, 1940).

124 Cf. Peter Selg, *Sterben, Tod und geistiges Leben. Die Kondolenzbriefe Ita Wegmans und das Todesverständnis der anthroposophischen Geisteswissenschaft*. Dornach, 2005.

125 Letter from Ita Wegman to Lilly Schäppi, Ascona, May 30, 1942.

126 Letter from Ita Wegman to Gertrud Schaub, Ascona, June 12, 1941.

127 In Liane Collot d'Herbois' notable description: "Sometimes, someone might approach her [Ita Wegman] with an inflated sense of self-importance and then leave with a sense of his or her own ridiculousness, able to laugh heartily with her about it. Because of her wise sense of humor, she was always able to have the right distance from everything and to look at the problems objectively from that distance. She was able to radiate brightness all around her, but because she also knew evil, it was possible for her to objectify it as well; and through her knowledge of human beings, her abundance of light and her wise sense of humor, she had the gift of being able to help and to heal in the true sense of the words.... Air—Frau Wegman created air; air filled with sunlight. She created movement. You could be carried along by her movement, because the conditions of movement in her being gave you the feeling that anything was possible. This movement was also evident in the way that she spoke, in the words that painted, in a completely unintellectual sense, with words; and this is how she conducted her conversations and held her lessons" ("Ita Wegman," 13, original in English).

128 "For a while, we had a young cat in the Casa, a very lively little creature who followed Dr. Wegman around whenever it could. Like all cats, this one also had a great affinity for the spiritual, and one day it decided to visit Dr. Wegman's Sunday lecture. She was the first one in the room. But the people who came in did not want to have her there and chased her around, and finally the poor little thing was tossed out the door. It reentered with other audience

members, and again it was hunted down and tossed out. Then the door opened and Frau Dr. Wegman stepped in, wearing a long dress, as she always did when she gave a lecture. And she smiled down at the cat that came in with her, sticking close to her heels. The cat sat under Dr. Wegman's stool and did not move until the lecture was over" (Liane Collot d'Herbois, *"Jeder, der strebt, ist mein Freund." Persönliche Erinnergungen an Ita Wegman*, 111).

129 "The most valiant doctor / of the twentieth century / Dr. Ita Wegman"—with these words, Guenther Wachsmuth wrote a dedication to Ita Wegman in May 1924 in a book of selected texts from "a pre-Christian forerunner," Hippocrates (*Hippokrates: Erkenntnisse*. Edited and translated by Theodor Beck (Jena: Eugen Diedrichs, 1907]). Now in the Ita Wegman archive.

130 Liane Collot d'Herbois, "Erinnerungen an Ita Wegman" [Memories of Ita Wegman], *50 Jahre Ita Wegman-Fonds für soziale und therapeutische Hilfstätigkeiten*, (Ostern, 1993), 40.

131 Letter from Ita Wegman to Anni Ruhtenberg, Ascona, May 27, 1940.

132 Letter from Ita Wegman to Erich Kirchner, Ascona, Nov. 29, 1941.

133 Letter from Ita Wegman to Erich Kirchner, Ascona, Jan. 23, 1943.

134 Letter from Ita Wegman to Erich Kirchner, Ascona, Nov. 3, 1941.

135 Ita Wegman used this concept in a letter to Clémence M. Hausamann (Ascona, Mar. 9, 1942), to whom she described the initiative with the following words: "What is occupying us quite a bit currently is our intention to take war-ravaged children in at the 'the Motta' in Brissago. I am therefore trying to interest people in this and have already received some sponsorship that has allowed me to take on a few children. But I would like, if possible, to gather a nice group of them, to give these children the best that I can give them for three months—not just in terms of nourishment and climate, but also spiritual guidance. I believe that this is the absolute best thing that we could do for the future. I am including a newsletter about it with this letter. Read through it. Perhaps you know a few people who might be interested in this."

136 Letter from Ita Wegman to Werner Pache, Ascona, Mar. 22, 1941. In an earlier letter to Helen Eugster, Wegman stressed that she was absolutely not thinking of developing the Motta in Brissago into a proper curative education institute, because "as a curative education institute, one can really only think of it as a place where children who need a different climate could occasionally come for some period of time. A long-term curative education institute with all of its trappings is not possible here. It is too far removed from

the world; even for those in need of curative education, it is not good to live an isolated life for too long" (July 4, 1940).

137 "Once Ita Wegman was invited by a friend to have coffee in a restaurant on the Piazza in Ascona. Switzerland at the time was full of spies; they were seeking each other out in droves and there were many murders. While the two women were sitting, having their coffee, Ita Wegman's friend suddenly leaned forward and whispered, 'Do you see that man, Frau Doctor, he is a spy.' 'A what? What are you saying that he is?' Ita Wegman replied in her typically loud voice. Her friend whispered again in her ear, 'A spy, Frau Doctor—the man there is a spy!' 'Where?' asked Ita Wegman in a loud, clear voice. 'Where is there a spy?' And all of the men's faces in the room disappeared behind their newspapers" (Liane Collot d'Herbois, *"Jeder, der strebt, ist mein Freund": Persönliche Erinnerungen an Ita Wegman*, 111).

138 A few weeks after this renewed immersion in the city where she had once studied and worked, Wegman reported to van Deventer that she intended to rent an apartment there as a retreat from her medical activities, "and also to connect us more with Zürich than we have been in the past." Further substantiating that point, even if only in a brief intimation of it, Wegman wrote, "During my last visit there, I could once again sense the great international train that is Zurich, and I had the feeling of some sort of karma that could not be worked out and was waiting on fulfillment.... I cannot remain here [in Ascona] forever, but going back to Arlesheim is also not the right thing for me" (July 6, 1942). Ita Wegman shared with Werner Pache twelve days later that she was thinking about "getting a room or a small two room apartment in Zürich in order to establish a stronger relationship with the place. There is a karma there that lies before me, and I want to grasp it once again" (July 18, 1942). One week later, she shared with him the news that she intended to realize her Zürich plan, "because it is absolutely essential to be in exchange with the spiritual streams found in Zurich" (July 25, 1942). For more on Wegman's period of study in Zürich as well as her practice and the clinic she founded there, see Zeylmans, vol. 1, 48–75; regarding the "spiritual streams found in Zürich," Wegman is reckoning more than a little bit with C. G. Jung and his followers, with whom she also spent time in Ascona and wrestled with spiritually (see below). She wrote about those followers in the previously cited letter to Werner Pache, just before discussing her Zürich plans: "There are many important things for me to do here [in Ascona] because a large wave is coming toward the Casa from

the outside world now, another encounter with Jung, whose people are always coming toward us."
139 Letter from Ita Wegman to Helen Eugster, Ascona, June 20, 1942. In Wegman's letter to Eugster, she went on to write of the "storm": "You are familiar perhaps with the elemental spirit of the 'storm,' the elemental beings that are bound up with the fate of humanity." As evidenced by something she wrote on the same day to Gertrud Schaub, Wegman was preoccupied at the Casa during this period of time with the great epics and tragedies of world literature and their connection with Rudolf Steiner's karma lectures: "And at the same time, [we] see the things that are happening now as the results of many things that were or were not done in earlier times" (ibid.).
140 Letter from Ita Wegman to Julia Bort, Arlesheim, Sept. 16, 1929.
141 No further documents have surfaced about the concrete work that Wegman did with Walter in Ascona. Ita Wegman's notebooks from this period of time offer mere traces of it, such as the review of a few individual cases of sickness. Wegman's correspondences also offer only sporadic indications of it; for example, Wegman wrote to van Deventer in October 1941: "Here are the cases of sicknesses that related to breathing. From the included copy of the letter to Dr. Marti [no longer extant] you will see how we divided them up. Try working with them. We will also send our work on them, which was actually intended for the Natura. As soon as I am up to it again, we will be going further" (Oct. 2, 1941). We do not know to what extent the conception and organization of the publications that Hilma Walter later undertook (see *Grippe, Encephalitis, Poliomyelitis. Zur Pathogenese und Behandlung. Mit fünfzehn Krankengeschichten* [Arlesheim, 1953]; *Der Krebs und seine Behandlung. Eine Sammlung von Krankengeschichten, mit Hinweisen von Rudolf Steiner* [Arlesheim, 1955]; *Abnormitäten der seelisch-geistigen Entwicklung in ihren Krankheitserscheinungen und den Behandlungsmöglichkeiten* [Arlesheim, 1955]; *Die sieben Hauptmetalle* [Arlesheim, 1965]; *Die Pflanzenwelt* [Arlesheim, 1971]) accorded with the work and conversations with Ita Wegman in Ascona.
142 Margarethe Kirchner-Bockholt, "Das Jahr 1924" (the year 1924). See also Hilma Walter, "Was ist und was will das Nerven-Nährpräparat?" in *Hefte des Ita Wegman-Fonds für soziale und therapeutische Hilfstätigkeiten* (1945). The "dietary nerve compound," which later had the name "Fragador," in the context of the larger production undertaken by the Cora company that was housed in one of the Motta buildings, was developed by Hilma

Notes

Walter, together with Ita Wegman, originally produced in the Casa and sent by Werner Pache to the Red Cross (see M. Helffenich, "Erinnerungen an die Casa Andrea Cristoforo und die Motta," in *50 Jahre Ita Wegman-Fonds für soziale und therapeutsiche Hilfstätigkeiten* [Ostern, 1993], 36).

143 When Liane Collot d'Herbois, who was working at the time in the curative education institute of Clent (England) with Fried Geuter and Michael Wilson, asked Ita Wegman for a letter of recommendation at the beginning of 1937 for a different curative education position in Ireland, Wegman answered her and her sister Ivonne with these words: "Of course I am ready to give Liane the best of references if she needs one and a request for one comes to me. May she succeed in finding the work that is out there for her and that she is now seeking in the hopes of gaining better material circumstances. I can well understand that! All the same, I must say that I will never cease to find it terrible that Liane is not simply painting and painting and painting some more. I saw several of her paintings behind glass in Clent, and I was so astonished all over again at how beautiful they are; a new form must be brought into the world through this art. Now, a new form such as this requires work and effort and sacrifice. Great artists never had money and could never have earned it—others had to do it for them. So do not forget, dear Liane and dear Ivonne, that you have friends and that you could always come to Arlesheim or to Tessin, if you wanted to, and *do nothing but paint*. Perhaps your plan to go to Ireland will succeed, but when I think of Liane, I always think more of a studio than of an institute for education" (Feb. 12, 1937). Liane Collot d'Herbois did not end up going to Ireland, but rather to Paris, where she, following an invitation from Wegman, worked on art in her house on rue de l'Assomption, painting with patients and making plant-based colors before she, once more through England, moved in the spring of 1940 to Ascona, and with that, put herself in close proximity to Ita Wegman. See Peter Selg (Walter Schneider, ed.), *Liane Collot d'Herbois. Werk und Leben—Work and Life*. Ittigen, 2013.

144 For more on Ita Wegman's relationship to visual art, see especially the essays by Liane Collot d'Herbois: "Ita Wegman" (1976); "A Lighter Aspect of the Personality of Ita Wegman" (1989; *Hefte des Ita Wegman-Fonds für sozile und therapeutische Hilfstätigkeiten*); and "Die Kapelle the Motta. Persönliche Erinnerungen an Ita Wegman" (1990; *Mitteilungen der Anthroposophischen Gesellschaft in Deutschland*, vol. 173).

THE LAST THREE YEARS: ITA WEGMAN IN ASCONA, 1940–1943

145 Liane Collot d'Herbois, "Die Kapelle the Motta. Persönliche Erinnerungen an Ita Wegman," 202.
146 Liane Collot d'Herbois, "Ita Wegman," 14 (original in English).
147 Letter from Ita Wegman to Anni Viehoff, Arlesheim, Sept. 21, 1940.
148 For example, in a letter to Werner Pache, Wegman described the encounter of an eight-year-old kleptomaniac boy from France with one of children visiting the Motta in words that show how friendly, attentive, interested, and sensible Wegman was in her awareness of the colorful and eye-opening life of the curative education community: "The boy is already beginning to feel a little bit at home, particularly since a blond girl has come to the Motta—Christiane, here for a short stay, who came with Lucie and Angela Wullschläger; the child has a sweet face, and the boy is absolutely crazy about her, has eyes for no one else but her and follows her around like a puppy dog. It is indeed strange to observe how something like this arises so strongly for a child, this draw toward a higher being—for that is how he looks at her, as though she is a magical being of light. He is already saying things like, *'c'est très bête de retourner maintenant,'* and does not want to hear about the fact that he has to leave [soon]" (July 18, 1942). A few weeks earlier, Ita Wegman had introduced Werner Pache to another boy, also eight years old, who had gotten so unruly in his parents' house that he had to leave: "You, Herr Pache, would take great delight in this boy, because in him you can see the expression of an interesting collision of the kinds of longings that such children bring down from the spiritual world, hoping to find them on Earth, with the disappointment of finding oneself in the midst of chaos rather than those longed-for realities" (July 1, 1942).
149 "4/22/1941: A difficult conversation with Frau Dr. Wegman in Ascona: she wants to have the children, with whom she is karmically connected, near her" (Werner Pache's diary).
150 "What warmth and fullness accompanied every step that she took on the piece of ground that embraces the Motta. How she delighted in the blossoms of every tree, just as she showed warm interest in the destiny of every person she encountered; whether pupil or colleague, she came toward them with joy, often surprising them. She refreshed and encouraged us all simply by being there" (Charlotte Fiechter, "Die Urnen-Kapelle der 'the Motta' in Brissago, Tessin," in *Hefte des Ita Wegman-Fonds für soziale und therapeutische Hilfstätigkeiten* [Michaeli, 1990], 8).
151 Nora von Baditz, "Ascona," in *Erinnerungen an Ita Wegman*, 66.
152 Letter from Ita Wegman to Werner Pache, Ascona, Feb. 28, 1941.

153 In prior years, Ita Wegman had corresponded constantly with A. Simons—Ben's very concerned Jewish grandfather, who lived in Scheveningen—about the situation of his handicapped grandchild in an increasingly threatening world. When World War II broke out, she sent him, for example, the following letter:

Arlesheim, Sept. 2, 1939
Dear Herr Simons!
　　I am writing to set you at ease about Ben. Should danger threaten us, we have taken all the necessary steps to be ready to go to a region in the middle of Switzerland or to Ascona in Tessin, where there will never be any battles, since it is in a valley. We could also reach higher ground quickly from there, if needed.
　　I am writing so that you can set your mind at ease.
　　It would perhaps be good if you were to write me a letter in which you gave me complete authority to do what is necessary for Ben's safety. In such times, one must always have all the papers and documents in order. You do not need to do anything except give me full power to take whatever steps I consider necessary for Ben's safety.
　　Everything is very quiet here; things are prepared, and neutrality will be protected.
　　I hope this finds you well.
　　With friendly greetings, to your wife as well
　　[signed] Dr. I. Wegman

154 Letter from Ita Wegman to Bendit Loeb, Ascona, Jan. 27, 1941.
155 Letter from Ita Wegman to Sidonie von Nostitz, Ascona, Jan. 27, 1941.
156 Letter from Ita Wegman to Walter Rummel, Ascona, July 8, 1940.
157 Letter from Ita Wegman to Jules Sauerwein, Ascona, Aug. 16, 1942.
158 Letter from Ita Wegman to Werner Kaelin, Ascona, June 26, 1942.
159 Letter from Ita Wegman to Gabrielle Boethius, Ascona, Nov. 16, 1940.
160 Letter from Ita Wegman to Heide Woog, Ascona, June 12, 1941.
161 Letter from Ita Wegman to Gabrielle Boethius, Ascona, Mar. 12, 1941.
162 Letter from Ita Wegman to Sesselja Sigmundsdottir-Svensson, Ascona, June 14, 1941.
163 Asked during a telephone call by a colleague (Meta Albrecht) who had returned to Arlesheim on short notice, to supply, if possible, the new and provisional location with further spiritual-scientific

literature, as well as supplies or clothing, Wegman gave instructions to do so from Ascona immediately, writing to Werner Pache, "These are unusually courageous people—there is no other way to put it—and we must do everything we can to help them. So I ask you heartily to take these things on. Everything is much more difficult to manage from here. Purchase some books from the press in Dornach and put them on my account. They do not have any of the recent publications [in La Plume]. And perhaps a few individual lectures as well. I thought of the "shell" cycle (CW 145, *The Effects of Esoteric Development.* Hudson, NY: Anthroposophic Press, 1997), which is being worked with in Arlesheim right now and that we are also going through here. It came out recently. Perhaps also a Gospel of Mark, which you do not have, I believe. And maybe something for Easter as well, which is fast approaching. Have a look at what you think is best—I do not know what else has come out. If Fräulein Albrecht can take supplies or clothing with her, then we could send some clothing and probably also some chocolate and cheese, which is fairly easy to transport" (Jan. 27, 1941). One day later, Ita Wegman reported to Gabrielle Boëthius in Sweden how dramatic it had been to get Hanna Lissau and Meta Albrecht, as well as some of their children, out of Paris a half year before as foreigners without any papers, trying to leave a city threatened by the approach of German troops: "They had to wait for permission to leave. Meanwhile, things kept progressing, until finally, two days before the catastrophe, without any sort of authorization, they get a space on the last car of the last train and rode directly to Toulouse." Wegman's letter ended with the words: "Things are hard for them; but in spite of that, they were able to carry on the work, and I am very proud of these unusually courageous people who pull through despite all of the difficulties they encounter and will now establish a new center of the work in the south" (Jan. 28, 1941). For more on the flight from Paris and the beginning of the Château d'Aguzan in La Plume, see also Meta Albrecht, "Vala Bérence: Bilder eines Lebens," in *Neues kommnt nicht von selbst. Erinnerungen an die Jahre der Aufbauarbeit der Heilpädagogik*, edited by Rüdiger Grimm (Dornach, 1999), 156; for more on Hanna Lissau, see below.

164 Letter from Ita Wegman to Karl König, Ascona, June 9, 1941.
165 Letter from Ita Wegman to Madeleine van Deventer, Ascona, Sept. 9, 1941.
166 Letter from Ita Wegman to Georg Mortiz von Sachsen-Altenburg, Ascona, Jan. 15, 1941. In this detailed piece of writing to the prince,

whom Wegman had accompanied on an extended journey through the Balkans in 1939, shortly before the outbreak of World War II, and with whom she had also been in Palestine in 1934, she writes regarding Gnadenwald: "You know that I have a weakness for this area and therefore would have liked to established the sanatorium there, that we might then have a connection to the East from there. This lives so strongly in me, just as strongly as the thought that I wanted to take that trip through the Balkans right before the start of the war. It was absolutely the last moment, and when I think back on all of it, I would not want to have missed anything that we experienced on that trip. I continue to think that in the midst of everything there, there are many possibilities for the German spirit. You are a part of that as well, dear prince, and that is why it would also be quite beautiful later if you travel to Gnadenwald often and play a part in creating a place for me there where I could make medicine with Hauschka and Stavenhagen. It has become very clear to me—precisely because the two of them are not here—just how spiritually connected I am with the two of them, and that this connection should continue into the future. For the time being, I do not believe that I should return to Arlesheim, but rather continue things there."

167 Letter from Ita Wegman to Nurse Katja Brühl, Ascona, Aug. 6, 1941.

168 Letter from Ita Wegman to Nurse Eva Vitzthum von Eckstaedt, Ascona, Oct. 1, 1941.

169 See also Peter Selg, 96. The documentation by Uwe Werner (*Anthroposophen in der Zeit des Nationalsozialismus* [Munich, 1999]) is indirectly illuminating in terms of how clearly Wegman, with her lucid knowledge of National Socialism and her ability to act with both initiative and intelligent strategy, differentiated herself from the majority of anthroposophists at the time. In this, Wegman not only proved advantageous to her numerous international contacts during her lifelong participation in the historical-political processes—her precise and ever-deepening knowledge of Steiner's indications also served her in this—but also benefitted her own progress on the path of esoteric training.

170 Letter from Ita Wegman to Werner Pache, Ascona, Jan. 13, 1943. In Nora von Badtiz's unpublished records of Ita Wegman's years in Ascona from the year 1957 (*Die drei Jahre*), she remarks, in regard to the transition from 1942 to 1943, "One could hear, in intimate conversations with her, that she wants to move toward the Germans. 'I want to tell them something, to whisper in their ears, *Be*

strong, do not let yourselves be wiped out. If that happens, humanity will lose its "I.""

171 Letter from Ita Wegman to Erich Kirchner, Ascona, Aug. 26, 1941.
172 By 1936, Hanna Lissau was already occupied with the founding and opening of the small curative education center in Paris's rue de l'Assomption and had worked with Vala Bérence there; later she then returned to the Sonnenhof, where her sister also worked.
173 Letter from Ita Wegman to Werner Pache, Ascona, Dec. 15, 1939.
174 Letter from Ita Wegman to Jules Sauerwein, Ascona, Sept. 10, 1942.
175 See Peter Selg, 107.
176 Letter from Ita Wegman to Madeleine van Deventer, Ascona, Sept. 7, 1942.
177 Letter from Ita Wegman to M. Moojen, Ascona, July 3, 1941. Wegman writes in detail, "The last news was that Bock is in a concentration camp. It all goes back to the fact that they want to be sure that Communism is not secretly active somewhere in Germany, and since people think Anthroposophy is either connected with Freemasonry (because it is spiritual) or with Communism (because it is social), these measures are being taken wherever there is any suspicion, thanks to Himmler, who is heading up everything instead of Hess (who is of course much more spiritual), and to Hauer's (who is an outspoken hater of Anthroposophy) efforts to churn things up. Perhaps this is a sort of Last Judgment that is now occurring."
178 Letter from Ita Wegman to Susanne Lissau, Arlesheim, Sept. 9, 1942. Hanna Lissau died in the concentration camp of Auschwitz-Birkenau on Oct. 14, 1942 (information courtesy of Dr. Krzysztof Antończyk, head of the Digital Repository, Memorial and Museum, Auschwitz-Birkenau, Poland).
179 See Werner Pache, *Diary*.
180 Madeleine van Deventer, cited in Emanuel Zeylmans, vol. 2, 242.
181 Margarethe Bockholt, 45.
182 Letter from Ita Wegman to Werner Kaelin, Ascona, Mar. 9, 1942.
183 Cited in Nik Fiechter, letter to Emanuel Zeylmans van Emmichoven, Mar. 5, 1982.
184 Letter from Ita Wegman to Madeleine van Deventer, Ascona, July 8, 1940.
185 Letter from Ita Wegman to Werner Pache, Ascona, Feb. 5, 1943. Werner Pache made notes on Jan. 1, 1932, on a conversation with Ita Wegman about the debates in Dornach and had recorded, with abbreviated words, her answer to his question, "What will become of the institutions if we are thrown out of the society?": "Until

then, keep working for the Goetheanum, as though this were an impossibility. For as long as possible, maintain the resolve that Frau Dr. and we will remain at the Goetheanum. If this proves impossible, then Hitler will come to power, or vice versa."

186   Letter from Ita Wegman to Walter Rummel, Ascona, July 8, 1940.
187   Letter from Ita Wegman to Wilhelm Goyert, Ascona, Jan. 17, 1941.
188   Liane Collot d'Herbois, "Ita Wegman," 3.
189   "Here, I was able to meet many people who came toward me, fresh and unburdened, from the Goetheanum." And: "It is such a shame how much things are going awry because the Anthroposophical Society is not functioning and my work is somehow being constantly wiped out or shoved into the background. As a result, various people are not coming to me" (Apr. 27, 1942 to Madeleine van Deventer).
190   See also Rudolf Steiner, *Das Schicksalsjahr 1923 in der Geschichte der Anthroposophischen Gesellschaft,* CW 259.
191   Letter from Ita Wegman to Anni Ruhtenberg, Ascona, Aug. 10, 1940.
192   Letter from Ita Wegman to M. Moojen, Ascona, July 22, 1940.
193   Letter from Ita Wegman to Lilly Schäppi, Ascona, Aug. 17, 1942.
194   Letter from Ita Wegman to Anni Ruhtenberg, Ascona, Oct. 7, 1940.
195   Letter from Ita Wegman to Lilly Schäppi, Ascona, July 1, 1942.
196   Letter from Ita Wegman to Baron Hugo von Tinty, Ascona, Mar. 2, 1942.
197   Ita Wegman, cited in Werner Pache, *Diary.*
198   Erika Müller, "Drei Kriegsweihnachten in Ascona," in *Ita Wegmans Erdenwirken aus heutiger Sicht,* published by the Ita Wegman Fund for Social and Therapeutic Activity (Arlesheim, 1976), 38.
199   Madeleine van Deventer, *Brief an die Freunde nach dem Tode Ita Wegmans,* Arlesheim, Apr. 15, 1943.
200   "He [Rudolf Steiner] said at the time that he could not set foot in Ascona because of the unsavory machinations of certain occultists who ruled on the Monte Verita" (Schubert, 15).
201   Letter from Ita Wegman to Madeleine van Deventer, Ascona, Aug. 6, 1942.
202   This was the theme and title of the course requested by Daniel N. Dunlop ("True and False Paths of Spiritual Investigations") that Rudolf Steiner had held in Torquay in summer 1924 in Torquay and that Ita Wegman had attended. It was first published by Marie Steiner in 1927 as *Das Initiaten-Bewusstsein* (CW 243, *True and*

False Paths in Spiritual Investigation. London: Rudolf Steiner Press, 1985).
203 Letter from Ita Wegman to Madeleine van Deventer, Ascona, Aug. 1, 1941.
204 Liane Collot d'Herbois, "Ita Wegman," 13.
205 See especially Wegman's stirring essays on Michael in the weeks and months following Rudolf Steiner's death (in *An die Freunde* [Arlesheim, 1960]; selections in English: Ita Wegman, *Esoteric Studies: The Michael Impulse,* Temple Lodge, 2013.
206 Ita Wegman, "Notebook entry," (undated).
207 Letter from Ita Wegman to Anni Ruhtenberg, Ascona, Oct. 7, 1940.
208 Letter from Ita Wegman to Hilma Walter, Ascona, Sept. 30, 1941.
209 Letter from Ita Wegman to Margarethe Bockholt, Ascona, Sept. 30, 1941.
210 Letter from Ita Wegman to Madeleine van Deventer, Ascona, Nov. 29, 1941.
211 Letter from Ita Wegman to Madeleine van Deventer, Ascona, Dec. 8, 1941.
212 Letter from Ita Wegman to Werner Kaelin, Ascona, Jan. 18, 1941.
213 Letter from Ita Wegman to Madeleine van Deventer, Ascona, Dec. 21, 1941.
214 Letter from Ita Wegman to Werner Pache, Ascona, Dec. 23, 1941. One year earlier, Wegman had written in a different letter, "May this Christmastime and its 13 Holy Nights give you what humanity needs so very much, namely the confidence in your soul that spirit will conquer materialism; construction and not the lust for destruction, the sensible rather than the senseless will rule. This is spoken very broadly, dear Frau Fellerer, but you will surely understand that behind these words stand the powerful reality of Rudolf Steiner's Spiritual Science, and that there must be people who consciously stand against the lust for destruction currently sweeping the world" (letter to M. Fellerer, Dec. 26, 1940).
215 Letter from Ita Wegman to Nurse Wilma Kröncke, Ascona, Jan. 15, 1941.
216 Letter from Ita Wegman to Hilma Walter, Arlesheim, Jan. 28, 1942.
217 "Ita Wegman," in *Hefte des Ita Wegman-Fonds* (1976), 4. In the report on the lectures that Madeleine van Deventer gave in various cities on the occasion of Ita Wegman's hundredth birthday in 1976, van Deventer noted that the sentence cited here—"I want to allow all of Anthroposophy to flow anew through my soul"—was

something that Ita Wegman said in the last weeks of her life, as were the words: "Rudolf Steiner is my only spiritual teacher. May the only thing said about me at my cremation be that I always wanted to serve Rudolf Steiner."

218 In her descriptions of various Mystery schools, Wegman would often refer to her travels and organized evenings during which she would show a number of her own well-organized photographs, housed today in the Wegman Archive. In 1941 she mentioned in a letter that she also maintained a connection to the historical events and processes. In a noteworthy piece dated June 12, 1941, she writes, "Recently we have been going through the things that came to us from the events in places like Greece and the Balkans. It seemed to me as though, by touching on the contact of the German spirit with all of these countries, the things connected with Greece and with the Mysteries there came alive in me; all of it came alive again, and I feel these things inside of myself, more alive than they were before" (Letter to Heide Woof).

219 Werner Pache heard one of these descriptions around Easter in 1942 and made notes for himself about it in his diary: "Frau Dr. Wegman was doing active spiritual work. In the middle of April, I was there when she spoke about Christian Rosenkreutz. Thoroughly penetrated."

220 According to her notebooks and letters, as well as Werner Pache's diary, Ita Wegman spoke on Mar. 30, 1941, in Arlesheim about Rudolf Steiner's life against the backdrop of the newly emergent cultural epoch that was renewed in him; then, a year later (on Feb. 26, 1942) between Steiner's birthday and his day of christening, she spoke in Ascona about aspects of his life and work: "I did it on that day because two patients were there—two Swiss women—who had never heard of Dr. Steiner and were very interested in him. It is remarkable how two people who had never heard of Dr. Steiner before could be brought completely into Anthroposophy in the course of 14 days. The time for this has truly come" (letter to Anni Ruhtenberg, Feb. 28, 1942). A few weeks later, on the anniversary of Steiner's death on Mar. 30, she spoke again in the Casa about "intimate events during the last hours of Rudolf Steiner's life" (letter to Erich Kirchner, Mar. 31, 1942). In Wegman's notebook, there are only a few notes for another speech on the same day, which was to begin with the words: "This morning it was necessary to speak of the intimate experience of the last hours of R. S. [Rudolf Steiner's] life. Of course, such accounts are subjective, for they are bound up with the soul experience of the people who experienced these things

personally. But they have a value for humanity, because important teachings are connected with these personal experiences—teaching that come out of the depth of R.S. [Rudolf Steiner's] Spiritual Science." No copies of prepared manuscripts exist of these last great lectures by Ita Wegman about Rudolf Steiner. In Werner Pache's diary, one finds only a few short notes about the lecture on Mar. 30, 1941, as well as noteworthy entries from Feb. 26, 1932, in which Pache recorded Wegman's remarks on Steiner's last birthday on Feb. 27, 1924: "He wanted to be completely alone. Frau Dr. Steiner was away. Wachsmuth, who regularly came at 5 o'clock with a folder full of business, was probably there as usual, and perhaps also Steffen, briefly, and Dr. Noll. Otherwise he was alone. He sat in his chair and read the letters that had come; there was a knock now and again and somebody would come in with flowers. Frau Dr. Wegman would then go to bring them in, show them to him, at which point he would look at them through his glasses and say, 'Very beautiful,' and then go back to reading. Then Frau Dr. Wegman gave him a leather folder as a gift—a very practical one with many pockets. He liked that very much and immediately began to put the letters inside and use it. He was already very tired, but there must still have been some hope that he would turn the corner. This expectation was there until the very end. That is probably why he would always say that he was meant to carry on. Otherwise it would not make any sense that during these days, indeed on Frau Dr. Wegman's birthday, he said, 'It would be nice if we could go to Palestine sometime.' Work continued on the [medical] book up until a few days before his death. When he gave it to Frau Dr. Wegman with the final corrections, he said, 'Something great will come of this.' What he had always said before that point, that more could come about in the future, he did not say that time. Three days before his death, there was a noticeable change. From that point forward, he became very, very still and *deeply solemn*, as though he was thinking, 'The spiritual world has closed; there is nothing more to do and yet he still does not give up his life.'"

221 "What do we mean when we say Christian esotericism? Christian esotericism refers to the secret of the Christ becoming human. The secret of the death and resurrection of Jesus Christ; the teachings of the resurrection and the secret of the Ascension" (Notebook entry; undated).

222 Erika Müller, "Drei Kriegsweihnachten in Ascona," in *Ita Wegmans Erdenwirken aus heutiger Sicht*, published by the Ita Wegman Fund for Social and Therapeutic Activity (Arlesheim, 1976), 37.

223 Letter from Ita Wegman to Antonie Manzoni, Ascona, Jan. 20, 1941.
224 Ita Wegman, Notebook entry (undated).
225 See also Rudolf Steiner's lectures from June 1906, especially the lecture given on June 1, 1906, collected in *Kosmogonie* (CW 94, *An Esoteric Cosmology: Evolution, Christ & Modern Spirituality*. Great Barrington, MA: SteinerBooks, 2008). In the same book, one will find the description offered in Berlin on Feb. 26, 1906, the lecture given in Leipzig on July 11, 1906, and the remarks in Munich from Nov. 4, 1906, which Ita Wegman also clearly pointed out to Liane Collot d'Herbois in Ascona and with which she lived and did intensive spiritual work, as her notebooks clearly show. Rudolf Steiner names the seven steps or "trials" of the Christian initiation: "feet washing," "flagellation," "the crown of thorns," "crucifixion," "mystical death," "burial/resurrection," and "ascension," and describes them as spiritual experiences to be undergone. If one looks closely at the experiences that befell Ita Wegman in the 1930s in Dornach, as well as her increasingly altered attitude toward them, it becomes clear that Wegman had undergone the course that Steiner described ever more consciously. And with this, the third step, the "crown of thorns," of which Steiner said in Berlin, "This step is connected not only with pain, but with the contempt of one's fellow human beings. One must struggle to have the strength to tolerate the effacement when no one but oneself is there to give one courage and support; one has the sense of being completely worthless, and yet one must remain upright. So must this be experienced. Such a trial lives itself out in the spiritual world as the experience of the crown of thorns: the human being sees itself wearing that crown of thorns" (p. 204 in the German edition). This is a development that found its fulfillment and perceptible expression in Ascona.
226 "One day, a woman came and was astonished at the inner light that streamed out of the being of Ita Wegman. 'How can you be so happy? I have never experienced such happiness,' she asked. 'Oh, I can tell you that,' she answered, 'once I was able to forgive everything that had ever been done to me, this sense of happiness came over me'" (Nora von Baditz, *Die drei Jahre*). Nora von Baditz added her own perspective on this conversation: "She [Ita Wegman] comforted and illuminated everyone around her with this unprecedented happiness."
227 Madeleine van Deventer, "Ita Wegman," 4.

228 Ita Wegman, cited in Liane Collot d'Herbois, "Die Kappel in 'the Motta' (Brissago)," in *Hefte des Ita Wegman-Fonds für soziale und therapeutische Hilfstätigkeiten* (Arlesheim, 1990), 12. "The only thing that gives life is devotion, devotion to the Mystery of Golgotha" (original in English).

229 Liane Collot d'Herbois, 10 (original in English). In two other very similar reports written and published at around the same time, Collot d'Herbois went into her connection with the restoration of the chapel, which was personally initiated by Ita Wegman, in more detail. Regarding the chapel, she writes, "For my whole life, I have been thankful that I was given the task of painting the walls of the chapel in Brissago, in which Ita Wegman's ashes will be housed after her death. When she asked me to draft some sketches, she explained to me that the place where her ashes would be housed would establish a connection to the Earth so that she would be able to continue to work in the earthly world from the spiritual one" ("Die Kapelle Motta. Persönliche Erinnerungen an Ita Wegman," in *Mitteilungen aus den anthroposophischen Arbeit in Deutschland*, vol. 173 [Michaeli, 1990], 202). Also, "Regarding the frescos in the chapel in Brissago, I would just like to say the following: after the content of them had been discussed with Frau Dr. Wegman and she had approved the sketches, I asked her why she wanted a protected place on Earth for her ashes. The answer was that Dr. Steiner had told her that the little spot where a person's ashes are housed becomes a central point from which he or she can radiate outward across the Earth, so that those who have passed on can continue their work through this special place" ("Ita Wegman," 15; original in English).

230 Ita Wegman, notebook entry (undated).

231 Ludwig Polzer-Hoditz, *In memoriam Frau Dr. Ita Wegman*, cited in Emanuel Zeylmans, vol. 3, 412.

232 Ita Wegman, notebook entry, Dec. 31, 1940.

233 Letter from Ita Wegman to Marianne Bischoff, Ascona, Dec. 12, 1940.

234 Letter from Ita Wegman to Madeleine van Deventer, Ascona, Jan. 20, 1941.

235 Ita Wegman, *Einleitungsansprachen zu Klassenstuden in Paris und Hamburg* (manuscript), cited in Emanuel Zeylmans, vol. 3, 63. Werner Pache also made notes in his diary about Ita Wegman's remarks at a gathering on Jan. 27, 1935, where, after a long pause in relation to this topic, the future of holding class lessons was

Notes

addressed: "Finally a decision to offer the class lessons again, but in a freer form. This is a start."

236 A trace (!) of these events and the intentions of Wegman that they express can also be found in later remarks by Liane Collot d'Herbois, who writes in regards to the class lessons: "Her [Wegman's] seriousness could be seen when she gave the First Class. She was only ready to proceed when all of the discord between us had been laid aside, and as a result she often had to wait a long time" ("Erinnerungen an Ita Wegman," *50 Jahre Ita Wegman-Fonds für soziale und therapeutische Hilstätigkeiten* [Ostern, 1993], 40). The extant documents do not provide definite evidence for how often Ita Wegman led the class during her last three years, in spite of her refusal to do so at Christmas in 1940. Individual class lessons on the occasion of her short visits to Arlesheim (for example in Mar. and June 1941) are documented. In Ascona, it seems that Wegman did not hold any class lessons at all until the summer of 1942, although she indicated to Mien Viehoff on Apr. 15, 1940, "we will certainly do that," and she would organize class lessons during her anticipated stay at the Casa. But then she decided to start, and in a letter from June 20, 1942, she wrote, "I have a small wish to be able to hold class lessons here, but must have a sufficient number of capable people who could participate, and I do not want to set a time before I know how many I can count on" (Letter to Gertrud Schaub). According to van Deventer's notes, at least one class lesson took place at the Casa on Michaelmas 1942 (see below).

237 Ita Wegman, notebook entry (Dec. 31, 1941). In Wegman's notebook, this is followed by the word "Die" ("The") on the next line, and then the text breaks off without any continuation. With..., we mark annexations by the author of this book; the marking (...) reproduces marginal notes from Ita Wegman herself. Missing punctuation has been added.

238 Letter from Ita Wegman to Werner Pache, Ascona, Jan. 13, 1943.

239 Madeleine van Deventer, "Die Rhythmen im Werdegang der Klinik," in *Hefte des Ita Wegman-Fonds für soziale und therapeutische Hilfstätigkeiten* (1971), 11. In this essay, van Deventer also draws attention to the fact that this Michaelic speech on the future occurred exactly *twenty-one years* after the founding of the clinic in Arlesheim: "The clinic has just finished its twenty-first year."

240 Madeleine van Deventer, *Zur Zeit des Zweiten Weltkrieges*.

241 In spring 1942, Werner Pache summed up the situation during the last few months at the Clinical Therapeutic Institute with these words: "Increasing fatality at the clinic. No turning the corner,

fewer patients, an increasing deficit. Frau Dr. Wegman is not interested and is not working to keep the people here—van Deventer, Kirchner, Rudolph and so on—from having to start all over again. It is all somewhat hopeless" (Diary).

242   Madeleine van Deventer, *Zur Zeit des Zweiten Weltkrieges*. Van Deventer continues her report here with these words: "I read the letter twice through and then tore it up into small pieces, unfortunately! At the time, I myself was too deeply enmeshed in the unsolvable problems of the moment."

243   Ita Wegman had worked for years with the accounts of St. Odilia and the Holy Grail and their connection to Arlesheim and to anthroposophic medicine and was connected in her destiny with them (see also Peter Selg, *Ita Wegman und Arlesheim*. Dornach, 2006). She evidently wrote a brief, straightforward introduction to the book of the legend in Dec. 1942: "The legend is...nothing other than a reflection of inner experiences that lead from ancient paganism to Christianity, but it is also a Christianity that is different than what it has become over the course of centuries" (letter to Margarethe Bockholt, Nov. 8, 1942). Ita Wegman had originally wanted Werner Pache to write this preface; she had repeatedly stressed to him the value of Baditz's text as well as the original version of the Odilia legend referenced by Rudolf Steiner: "It [the piece by Nora von Baditz] is unassuming, but it has a moral force and it could be very real, because Odilia—as Rudolf Steiner said—experienced the Christianizing period.... It is essential to take up this story once again, because all of that is reflected in Arlesheim, and—as Rudolf Steiner said—it was given as a kind of insight to certain people who then went on to found the anthroposophic movement in Arlesheim and Dornach" (Oct. 21, 1942). Despite Wegman's praise, Werner Pache kept his reservations about Nora von Baditz's text, which evidently caused Wegman to take matters into her own hands. The introductory text (a typewritten copy with handwritten remarks by Ita Wegman can be found in the Ita Wegman Archive) ultimately read as follows: "A breath of wonder surrounds the life of the holy Odilia. Her life stands under the sign of transformation, the transformation from ancient paganism to Christian culture, and this is how we must understand her legend. History tells us that she lived from 660 to 720. Her father Etticho was closely tied to the Merovingians and was much a man of his time, which was still largely pagan. The news of Christianity had already made its way from the South to the North, all the way to Ireland and Scotland. Etticho had not been moved by it. When a blind daughter was born to him, he considered

this a personal shame, and he cast her off. Now, at this point in the legend of Odilia, it is described how the 'one born blind' becomes the 'seeing one.' Odilia, blind from birth, represents the end of the pagan culture, whereas her father Etticho, who casts her off, is still much a part of pagandom. In her, the light breaks through; she binds herself to the Christian impulses and begins to see. The moment that she returns to her parents' house, having grown to maturity, she is unceasingly active in bringing about the end of the pagan culture that had found a significant seat on the Vosges mountains and in bringing about the rise of Christianity. She was able to do this with the help of the forces of love and through her tireless activity. It was a new, helpful force of love that worked in a holy manner and which she gave to the poor and to the sick. This was Christianity in its most beautiful form. This font of healing love that can be brought to consciousness within a human being is known as finding the Holy Grail. Back then, this Holy Grail was often spoken of. People understood the Holy Grail to be the transformative powers that are active within a human being and that can turn the darkness present within the soul into illumination. So it is lovely to know of a place that can be found in Elsass where ancient pagan culture was transformed into a seat for Christian love. There in the Vogesen, on the Odilienberg, the Christian cloister of Odilia was founded. It is worth it to visit this place. There you can find the traces of Irish wanderers who came down from the North to spread Christianity, not through the sword, but through one in whom dwelt the same forces of transformation that turn the darkness of the soul into holiness and healing activity. The relief of Odilia, carved into a column that also holds Etticho's charter for the construction of the cloister, speaks to the remains of an eloquent language. And so this little book, through a new retelling of the legend of the Holy Odilia who had the power to transform the soul, hopes to tell of how something very significant came into the world from this place." Ita Wegman published Baditz's version of the legend, along with her preface, in an initial run of 1,200 copies at the beginning of December 1942 under the title *Augen, die sehend wurden* [Eyes that began to see]. They sent it to many friends and sold it successfully at the cost of two francs, at the Christmas bazaars in Arlesheim and Ascona for example, but also in the following weeks: "We are still selling lots of the Odilia books" (Jan. 13, 1943, to Werner Pache). A children's home in Bern, whose director Hanna Schwab was in close contact with Werner Pache and Ita Wegman, took 250 copies. The work appeared under the same title on the regular book market (von Baditz, *Augen, die sehend wurden*) seventeen years after Wegman's death, published by the Melinger Verlag in Stuttgart, though without any indication of its initial publication in 1942 and without any attribution for the otherwise unaltered forward, the last text that Wegman prepared for a publication.

244 Rudolf Steiner, *Die Apokalypse des Johannes*, 37 (CW 104, *The Apocalypse of St. John: Lectures on the Book of Revelation*. London: Rudolf Steiner Press, 2004).

245 Ibid., 32.

246 Ibid., 74. "So we could say that gradually our culture will live into a culture of brotherly love in which a relatively small number of people will have understood the spiritual life or have prepared the spirit and sense of brotherly love. This culture will then parcel out a smaller group of people, and they will be the ones who survive the event that will have such a destructive effect on our [evolutionary] circle—the war of all against all. During this generally destructive occurrence, there will be individuals everywhere who rise above the rest of the warring humanity, individuals who have understood spiritual life and will form the foundation of a new and different epoch" (Ibid., 88).

247 See also the Paris lecture given on June 14, 1906, as well as Steiner's discussion surrounding it (CW 94, *An Esoteric Cosmology: Evolution, Christ & Modern Spirituality*. Great Barrington, MA: SteinerBooks, 2008). At the end of her life, Wegman engaged intensively with the spiritual strata and forces that Steiner thematized in this lecture, relating them to the events surrounding the Christ as well as the coming catastrophes in the natural world and in civilization. This is evidenced by her notebooks, by notes taken by Hilma Walter on her lectures, and particularly by Mien Viehoff's write-up of Ita Wegman's Casa lectures during the period of time from July 5, 1942 to Feb. 18, 1943.

248 Letter from Ita Wegman to Madeleine van Deventer, Ascona, Jan. 9, 1942. Liane Collot d'Herbois wrote in later remarks on Ita Wegman: "Before her death, she was very worried about what was to come. She spoke to me about the gift of prophecy, which comes from the sun, and one could assume that she knew what she was talking about." ("Erinnerungen an Ita Wegman" ["Memories of Ita Wegman"], in *50 Jahre Ita Wegman-Fonds für soziale und therapeutische Hilfstätigkeiten* [Ostern, 1993], 40.)

249 "How heavily do the prophetic visions of St. John weigh upon our minds, oppressive to experience in the midst of wartime experiences. Often, the things described went far beyond our ability to grasp them, and this would always cause Frau Dr. Wegman distress.

I remember that she said at the end of one evening that we had not gotten through that together, and she wanted to work with it again on the following day. And then it was another difficult struggle without a satisfying result. To be sure, it was another 'elevated time,' but nothing like the protected quiet of last year. Often Frau Dr. Wegman would step into the room with the gravest of expressions; often she would make that hand gesture, so characteristic of her, as though she wanted to brush a spider web away from her face" (Müller, see endnote no. 250). Werner Pache referred in his diary to a Christmas letter—no longer extant—from Ita Wegman from the same period, addressed to the colleagues at the Sonnenhof: "Frau Dr. Wegman wrote that the world situation seems very dire. One must think of miracles. In the cycle on the Gospel of St. John from Kassel, it says that one could indeed imagine that in our time, a person with the power of Christ might be walking among us; but those who would have the *strength of belief* in him are few and far between, and he would not be able to bring about the transfer of things from one side to the other through the influence of soul. And so now, if *miracles* are to happen, there must be people who have the *strength to believe* in them. This is what we must practice" (Dec. 24, 1941).

250 Erika Müller, "Drei Kriegsweihnachten in Ascona," in *Ita Wegmans Erdenwirken aus heutiger Sicht*, published by the Ita Wegman Fund for Social and Therapeutic Activity (Arlesheim, 1976), 38.

251 Letter from Ita Wegman to Ruth Schmid, Ascona, Dec. 7, 1942.

252 Ita Wegman, notebook entry, Dec. 24, 1942.

253 In a report by Margarethe Kirchner-Bockholt, the doctor at the Motta, she writes in 1963, looking back at Christmas 1942, having described the Holy Night: "Now, it was typical on the first holiday morning to travel to Brissago and begin the children's day with a devotional celebration. Ita Wegman did this, despite her weakened state, even in the last year of her life, and she was able to reach a great number of the children. She spoke about the experience of Christmas in simple words, and the spirituality of this event was able to touch every heart in an unusually strong way as it came streaming in. Children whose understanding and external grasping of things is hindered by physical and mental handicaps often have a freer interchange with their soul-spiritual beings and thus have a surprising ability to take up spiritual matters that speak to them directly out of the experiences of their souls. A roughly sixteen-year-old boy who had been with us for a good bit of the year leapt up, grabbed her arm and said, 'You did that amazingly

well, Frau Doctor, amazingly well!'" ("Zum 20. Todestage von Ita Wegman," in *Das Seelenpflege-bedürftige Kind*, annual 10, no. 1 [Ostern, 1963], 5).

254   Ita Wegman, notebook entry (undated).

255   Rudolf Steiner, *Vorträge und Kurse über christlich-religiöses Wirken. Band V. Apokalypse und Priesterwirken*, 164 (CW 346, *The Book of Revelation: And the Work of the Priest*. London: Rudolf Steiner Press, 1998).

256   Ibid., 125.

257   Ibid., 87.

258   Erika Müller, "Drei Kriegsweihnachten in Ascona," in *Ita Wegmans Erdenwirken aus heutiger Sicht*, published by the Ita Wegman Fund for Social and Therapeutic Activity (Arlesheim, 1976), 38.

259   Nora von Baditz, "Ascona," in *Erinnerung an Ita Wegman*, 66.

260   Rudolf Steiner, *Die geistig-seelischen Grundkräfte der Erziehungskunst*, 152 (CW 305, *The Spiritual Ground of Education*. Hudson, NY: Anthroposophic Press, 2004).

261   Just five days after the Dornach General Assembly on Apr.14, 1935, Ita Wegman wrote to Walter Johannes Stein in London: "Now a strange thing has happened, dear Dr. Stein—you are still in the Society and I am not! Would you ever have imagined that?" (Arlesheim, Apr. 22, 1935). Other documents and correspondences confirm without a doubt that after Apr. 14, 1935, Ita Wegman did not see herself as an official member of the General Anthroposophical Society. This did not stop her from, for example, recommending to Eugen Kolisko in summer 1937 that he should establish a closer connection between his London-based "School of Spiritual Science" and the Anthroposophical Society in England, and to write, "I am always of the opinion that, although we have been pushed out of the Goetheanum, we are still the Anthroposophical Society, and indeed, a rather active part of it. And so long as it is possible, we must maintain this.... Dear Dr. Kolisko, perhaps you will laugh at this and say, 'I do not want anything to do with the Anthroposophical Society anymore,' and you will perhaps create something altogether different that does not have any connection with the Society. But I believe that, through Dr. Steiner, we are still in this Society and that it must gradually metamorphose. This metamorphosis must proceed such that a loose connection between the activities of different people comes about, but the Anthroposophical Society should be there as a larger Society—namely, as the community of the new Christians who want to take up the resurrected Christ as a reality in themselves. This does not need to be

said aloud, of course, but we must carry it within our hearts. This is the only way we will have true spiritual results. I hope that you will not be angry with me" (Arlesheim, June 10, 1937).

262 Letter from Ita Wegman to Helen Eugster, Ascona, Sept. 9, 1941.
263 Letter from Ita Wegman to Werner Pache, Ascona, Jan. 13, 1943.
264 Liane Collot d'Herbois, *"Jeder, der strebt, ist mein Freund."* Persönliche Erinnerungen an Ita Wegman, 113.
265 See also Hella Wiesberger, *Marie Steiner-von Sivers. Ein Leben für die Anthroposophie. Eine biographische Dokumentation.* Dornach, 1988, 493f.
266 Marie Steiner, "An die Mitglieder der Anthroposophischen Gesellschaft," in *Nachrichtenblatt*, 19 Annual, No. 51 (Dec. 20, 1942).
267 Letter from Ita Wegman to Werner Pache, Ascona, Jan. 13, 1943.
268 Cited in Zeylmans, vol. 2, 233.
269 Ibid., 234.
270 Wegman's relationship to The Christian Community was exceedingly positive, both in regard to its sacramental, ritual Mystery tasks, as well as her assessment of the personal bearers of the movement since 1922. Following her sickness and her experience in Palestine in 1934, this relationship only intensified and deepened. To Ita Wegman, who still spoke of the "superb cult" of The Christian Community in her later letters from Ascona, deeply regretted that because of geographical distance, acts of consecration by a priest of The Christian Community could only happen seldom, and then only on the occasion of someone's passing: "In November, Herr Professor Fiechter was here in Ascona in order to consecrate a body. After a long pause, we could once again allow this cult to work upon us, and we were very much affected by it and thankful that we have such a wonderful cult in The Christian Community; unfortunately, we can only participate so infrequently" (Letter to Ita Wyss, Dec. 19, 1942). Rudolf Steiner had once said, "It would be good, if Frau Dr. Steiner could gain an inner relationship to The Christian Community" (cited in Zeylmans, vol. 2, 226).
271 Liane Collot d'Herbois, *"Jeder, der strebt, ist mein Freund."* Persönliche Erinnergungen an Ita Wegman, 113.
272 Letter from Ita Wegman to Marie Steiner, Ascona, Feb. 15, 1943.
273 Madeleine van Deventer, *Autoreferat zu Vorträgen über Ita Wegman zum 100. Geburtstag 1976 in verschiedenen Städten* (Report on the lectures in various cities about Ita Wegman on her hundreth birthday).
274 Letter from Ita Wegman to Werner Pache, Ascona, Feb. 10, 1943.
275 Letter from Ita Wegman to Werner Pache, Ascona, Feb. 9, 1943.

276 Letter from Ita Wegman to Werner Pache, Ascona, Feb. 15, 1943.
277 Letter from Ita Wegman to Werner Pache, Ascona, Feb. 3, 1943.
278 Nora von Baditz referred to a conversation with Ita Wegman from Feb. 20, 1943, with these words: "On the last evening before her departure to Arlesheim: 'Do you believe that when I notice that the pulse of life is somewhere else, I would remain for an hour in Ascona?' she cried in a loud voice, and very quickly. When I said, 'No, Frau Doctor, I do not believe that,' she was visibly satisfied. After these words, she extended her hand to say, *'Stay healthy'*" (Nora von Baditz, *Die drei Jahre*).
279 Ibid.
280 Letter from Ita Wegman to Madeleine van Deventer, Ascona, Feb. 24, 1941.
281 In a summary report to van Deventer in Arlesheim written on Feb. 23, 1942, she wrote, "It was perhaps a little strange from your perspective that I left a day before my birthday. Well, I did not really mean anything by it. I always struggle with not having my birthday be all about me, and so this time I decided to disappear a little bit. But last year that was not so successful, and perhaps that is a good thing. After it became impossible to travel beforehand, my intention was to stay in Zürich through Sunday and then depart later. But in Zürich...it was so cold in the hotel and so uncomfortable, and the food was so bad, that I could not resolve to stay there and decided instead to take the train to Ascona, intending to spend Sunday at the 'Sole.' But of course that did not work, because as soon as we arrived somebody who had to broadcast the news of our arrival called up Frau Koch. I arrived late in the evening and wanted to go immediately to bed, only to find my room already decorated with tropical flowers, such as blooming mimosa and camellia and bougainvillea, as well as various letters and the like. At the time, your dear present from the clinic was also given to me. And so, as it turned out, the whole clinic was in my room until 12 at night, and that was really quite nice." During the following days, Wegman wrote a personal letter to every single worker at the Arlesheim Clinic who had signed the greeting card, and in most of the letters she included a detailed description of her unsuccessful journey to Zürich.
282 Madeleine van Deventer, "Die letzten Erdentage," in *Erinnerungen an Ita Wegman*, 68.
283 Ibid., 69.
284 Wegman's letter to Bockholt described the events in the greatest detail, while also showing a sense for the comedy of the happenings

and human entanglements—serious, if not existential conflicts—within the circles in Bern. Written just ten days before her death, Ita Wegman's report demonstrates yet again her active conduct in life, full of clearly directed energy, her intelligence in her work to follow through on her intentions, and her radiant joy as a confident, if not outright, sovereign woman among many men:

Arlesheim, Feb. 24, 1943
Dear Dr. Bockholt!

You are no doubt anxiously awaiting news; perhaps Kirchner wrote as well, but it is good that you are now receiving a report from me anyway. From the first day onward, I was very active. The first conversation with Löw [Ita Wegman's lawyer in Basel] on Sunday was very unsatisfying from my perspective. I saw all sorts of difficulties looming on the horizon. So Pache decided not to travel to Bern in the afternoon, but rather in the morning in order to be able to report to me, so that the further necessary steps could be taken immediately.

It became ever-more clear that motion on behalf of three people [meaning simultaneous naturalization applications for Pache, Kirchner, and Rudolph, which Ita Wegman had rejected from the beginning in favor of Pache] would not succeed and would actually risk a great deal. Dr Löw, who has a great sympathy for Rudolph—which I know, and you do as well, which is not to say that he does have sympathies for the rest of us, but there is a favoritism at work here, which has come about as a result of Rudolph's unique demeanor (which I can also understand)—wanted to bring Pache and Rudolph through first, and then do Kirchner later. He believed that Kirchner had the greatest chance, as the owner of the house, and that he was not in any immediate danger. Now, if you can understand this, it would not have been right psychologically to do that to Kirchner, because we would be skimming the cream off the top and indicating that we considered Rudolph to be the one that we could not do without and that we had to bring through. It was a situation full of bias, and everyone was not being fully honest.

Meanwhile, Pache and Löw went to Bern on Monday. There, Löw had a discussion with Herr Senti [the director of the immigration police for Basel and the surrounding area] because Löw brought forward the recommendation of the three men and encountered immediate resistance from Herr Senti, even though Senti had earlier received a letter from Herr Stämpfli with the recommendation to release Herr Pache regarding his future naturalization. Then Löw gradually had to adopt a different tone, and he succeeded in appeasing Senti so that he came to behave sympathetically toward Pache, which he had certainly intended to do from the get-go, had Löw not brought forward this unfortunate combination of applications. It all went just as I sensed it would; such things cannot be brought forward this way. Finally, Löw managed to get Senti to meet Pache and agree to speak with me possibly in the future. Senti immediately followed the suggestion of speaking with me and said that if it was not altogether too difficult for me, he would very much like to see me and speak with me again. Pache was able to communicate this to me immediately, which allowed me to go to Bern on Tuesday. I had already planned to go to the theater on Monday (the "Magic Island" by Sutermeister), just with Dr. van Deventer, because Kirchner had already seen it. Pache wanted to speak on the telephone again in the evening, after he had spoken again with Löw and Nurse Hanna—that would only have been possible after the play—and so we changed our plans a little bit, went to Basel, ate our evening meal there, Kirchner joined us, and while we sat in the theater, Kirchner could receive news from Pache by phone, because otherwise we could not have caught the last train in Basel after the play. In the meantime, I had also had a gathering with Rudolph, Kirchner and Dr. van Deventer in order to be clear about all of this with them, and at this conference, it was decided that I would travel to Bern alone, in order to be able to speak totally freely there and to do what I considered necessary, even though Löw recommended that it would be a human gesture to take the two men—and he mostly meant Rudolph—with me. I had no desire to do that and I justified my reasons to them, and the two of them understood me perfectly.

As we sat in Basel that evening, we looked for trains—I had no time to do that earlier—and Kirchner observed that the nine o'clock train stopped for 40 minutes in Olten and that I would have to change trains. Then everyone agreed that I should not do that alone, and that Kirchner would have to accompany me as far as Olten. There was no unsettling news from Bern, only confirmation that I should indeed take the nine-o'clock train. So, I took that one and Kirchner accompanied me. When I left the house at half past eight with Kirchner, I thought to myself, hopefully this does not lead to misunderstanding, if Rudolph sees us and thinks that Kirchner is being given preference and driving with me all the way to Bern. And lo and behold, to my great amazement—a half hour later, we sat in the train and who should appear? Rudolph, with a ticket to Bern. We were so perplexed that we were practically speechless. Kirchner explained why he was there and said, with large gestures, 'Now I have nothing more to do; Rudolph will accompany you from here,' and then he was gone. So there I sat in a crowded compartment between the two men and had to make the best of a bad situation in order to prevent a scene, because everyone was looking at us. After I had explained everything to Rudolph and said to him, 'now, good—accompany me as far as Olten, then please turn around and make things good with Kirchner,' I also said to him that I would do everything that was necessary, but also had to prioritize the things that were essential and important for our work, and then Rudolph was somewhat ashamed but otherwise quite reasonable; he understood everything, and so I rode alone to Bern after transferring in Olten, and there I was picked up by Pache. I have never felt more important than I did applying for the naturalization of these men, but still I had to laugh a little; I did not have any bad feeling about being able to see things through to a positive conclusion. This did happen, though not in the way that all three had expected. Senti would not speak at all about all three of them—on the contrary, the other two should withdraw (a letter from Rudolph had arrived in the meantime, which also was not good), for although he did not like to do it, his understanding of the situation at the curative education institute was that Pache was indispensable. I was then able to bring up that we would, at the very least, like to have a settlement for the other two men, because if they were called up to military service in Germany, then they would be able to return to Switzerland after their military service was over, provided they had settlements; this is actually why we wanted to have the settlements for them. Then he was able to assure me quite kindly that, "On the contrary, if someone does his duty and has worked here for many years and then wants to return to Switzerland, he will be gladly welcomed back into Switzerland." He said that so confidently and kindly, with Pache and Löw there as witnesses, that we were all quite relieved, and we could then say, "Well, Herr Senti, then the problems that are on our minds right now are actually solved." It is possible to bear a temporary deprivation of one's forces, but not an absolute one. Senti grew ever more friendly, and promised that our concerns would be dealt with generously.

Therefore, the result we achieved was that all forces were now focused on doing everything possible to get Pache released from the immigration police and to see to his subsequent naturalization. Now the two others—primarily Rudolph, since Kirchner still has not received a call from the military—must try to either be released from duty with a doctor's certificate or to serve in the garrison, and all of the necessary steps are being taken for this. Kirchner is also going to have his blood checked again. In Dr. van Deventer's estimation, Kirchner has the greater chance of being completely released from military duty. I will attempt to get Kirchner released by the General Counsel as someone whose service is indispensable to me as soon as there is time for it.

This is the short version of the long story of the threefold application. In the meantime, the mood has gotten better again, and I hope that everything else will go well, since we did well with this first step.

Fräulein Brauch has come again, and I will have a talk with her now. Yesterday morning, Eva Renate passed away.

Send everyone my best. Thank you for all of the good wishes and for the birthday donation.

It is hoped that everything is going well there.

With heartfelt greetings, Your I. Wegman

285 Letter from Ita Wegman to her friends at the Casa, Arlesheim, Feb. 24, 1943.
286 Madeleine van Deventer, cited in Zeylmans, Volume 2, 236.
287 "The doctor once said that Gandhi had the possibility of taking up Christianity within himself, and that through him, these Christian principles could be brought to India. Just think, if this were to occur, what tremendous significance it would have for India's evolution. But of course, he could not simply take Christianity in its external form, but rather Christianity in the form that Rudolf Steiner gave to us" (letter from Ita Wegman to Fried Geuter, Arlesheim, Oct. 29, 1931).
288 Madeleine van Deventer, "Die letzten Erdentage," in *Erinnerungen an Ita Wegman*, 70.
289 "What she hoped for the [political] future was a balance of forces, which would allow the spiritual to work most effectively on Earth. In every word spoken during these conversations, one was fully aware that *she* was ready to continue working with us on Earth, so long as the possibility existed for opposing the forces of downfall. In relation to this, she spoke the words cited above, 'the decision has not yet been made.' And she went on to say, 'If no spiritual work is possible in the near future, then I will die.' But the positivity with which she continued to look for the possibility of a victory of the spirit, even given the terrible desperate situation on Earth, is evidenced in other remarks, such as, 'I am always on the lookout for people who are still open for spiritual inspirations and who are also

in positions where people listen to them.' Then she described with great humor several dreams related to this search. For example, a listless man is sitting in front of a typewriter, completely sluggish. Dully he types letter after letter. Behind him is a voice that dictates to him. The voice becomes ever more penetrating and pushes him to greater efforts. Gradually, the sluggish man begins to wake up and writes faster and faster, until he is carrying out his work full of fiery haste. Then the voice behind him stops. And other, much more dramatic, often tender images followed. As she told these stories, although her expression was pained, Frau Dr. Wegman said, 'Ah, if only it were not so tragic, we could all laugh about it together'" (van Deventer, 70).

290 "Even late [into the final evening, Mar. 3, 1943] it was possible to speak about reports from Ascona and communicate all of the heartfelt greetings and well-wishes of her friends there. She had consciously accepted the fact that she would soon have to leave this plane. But it was a matter of her resolve to send greetings to all of her friends. More than once, she would simply add to her instructions, 'all, all.'...Then her thoughts would quickly turn to everyone she had been close to during her life, even though she no longer had the strength to name all of the individuals by name. But the fact that her instructions were to be understood in this sense seemed to be a great comfort to her" (Hilma Walter, *Der Lebensgang von Ita Wegman*, 18).

291 Madeleine van Deventer, *Zur Zeit des Zweiten Weltkriegs*.

292 Hilma Walter, 19.

Books in English Translation
by Peter Selg

ON RUDOLF STEINER:

Rudolf Steiner and Christian Rosenkreutz (2012)

Rudolf Steiner as a Spiritual Teacher: From Recollections of Those Who Knew Him (2010)

ON CHRISTOLOGY:

The Lord's Prayer and Rudolf Steiner: A Study of His Insights into the Archetypal Prayer of Christianity (2014)

The Creative Power of Anthroposophical Christology: An Outline of Occult Science · The First Goetheanum · The Fifth Gospel · The Christmas Conference (2012); with Sergei O. Prokofieff

Christ and the Disciples: The Destiny of an Inner Community (2012)

The Figure of Christ: Rudolf Steiner and the Spiritual Intention behind the Goetheanum's Central Work of Art (2009)

Rudolf Steiner and the Fifth Gospel: Insights into a New Understanding of the Christ Mystery

Seeing Christ in Sickness and Healing (2005)

ON GENERAL ANTHROPOSOPHY:

Spiritual Resistance and Overcoming: Ita Wegman 1933–1935 (2014)

The Last Three Years: Ita Wegman in Ascona, 1940–1943 (2014)

From Gurs to Auschwitz: The Inner Journey of Maria Krehbiel-Darmstädter (2013)

Crisis in the Anthroposophical Society: And Pathways to the Future (2013); with Sergei O. Prokofieff

Rudolf Steiner's Foundation Stone Meditation: And the Destruction of the Twentieth Century (2013)

The Culture of Selflessness: Rudolf Steiner, the Fifth Gospel, and the Time of Extremes (2012)

The Mystery of the Heart: The Sacramental Physiology of the Heart in Aristotle, Thomas Aquinas, and Rudolf Steiner (2012)

Rudolf Steiner and the School for Spiritual Science: The Foundation of the "First Class" (2012)

Rudolf Steiner's Intentions for the Anthroposophical Society: The Executive Council, the School for Spiritual Science, and the Sections (2011)

The Fundamental Social Law: Rudolf Steiner on the Work of the Individual and the Spirit of Community (2011)

The Path of the Soul after Death: The Community of the Living and the Dead as Witnessed by Rudolf Steiner in his Eulogies and Farewell Addresses (2011)

The Agriculture Course, Koberwitz, Whitsun 1924: Rudolf Steiner and the Beginnings of Biodynamics (2010)

Karl König's Path to Anthroposophy (2008)

On Anthroposophical Medicine and Curative Education:

I Am for Going Ahead: Ita Wegman's Work for the Social Ideals of Anthroposophy (2012)

The Child with Special Needs: Letters and Essays on Curative Education (Ed.) (2009)

Ita Wegman and Karl König: Letters and Documents (2008)

Karl König: My Task: Autobiography and Biographies (Ed.) (2008)

On Child Development and Waldorf Education:

I Am Different from You: How Children Experience Themselves and the World in the Middle of Childhood (2011)

Unbornness: Human Pre-existence and the Journey toward Birth (2010)

The Essence of Waldorf Education (2010)

The Therapeutic Eye: How Rudolf Steiner Observed Children (2008)

A Grand Metamorphosis: Contributions to the Spiritual-Scientific Anthropology and Education of Adolescents (2008)

Ita Wegman Institute
for Basic Research into Anthroposophy

PFEFFINGER WEG 1 A CH 4144 ARLESHEIM, SWITZERLAND
www.wegmaninstitute.ch
e-mail: sekretariat@wegmaninstitute.ch

The Ita Wegman Institute for Basic Research into Anthroposophy is a non-profit research and teaching organization. It undertakes basic research into the lifework of Dr. Rudolf Steiner (1861–1925) and the application of Anthroposophy in specific areas of life, especially medicine, education, and curative education. Work carried out by the Institute is supported by a number of foundations and organizations and an international group of friends and supporters. The Director of the Institute is Prof. Dr. Peter Selg.

www.ingramcontent.com/pod-product-compliance
Lightning Source LLC
Chambersburg PA
CBHW030856170426
43193CB00009BA/637